"*I Can, I Will & I Did: Lessons on Life, Love, and Leadership* offers a compelling snapshot into the decision-making process of a successful businesswoman facing life's unexpected and complex challenges."

—Lisa Gable, U.S. Ambassador, Best-selling Author of
Turnaround: How to Change Course When Things are
***Going South*, and Keynote Speaker**

"I'm so touched by Samina's memoir. We follow her journey as the only brown girl navigating the complexities of growing up in a strict Muslim household while trying to fit into the Western world. Through heartfelt storytelling, we witness her struggles with identity, belonging, and the quest for self-acceptance. The raw honesty and vulnerability in her reflections invite readers to empathize with her unique experiences, ultimately inspiring us to embrace our own multifaceted identities and the strength that comes from bridging cultural divides. This is a fully human story that is relatable for so many of us bridging multiple identities."

—Julie Castro Abrams, CEO and Chair of How Women
Lead, General Partner at How Women Invest

"Samina does a terrific job of capturing her life as an underdog. Her background is filled with walls, trapdoors, and uncertainties that mirror a real-life game of Chutes and Ladders. Based on all odds, she shouldn't have prevailed. Faced with a culture where women are second-class citizens, a mother who resented her daughter's dreams and chutzpah, and the premature loss of her beloved husband, Samina is the epitome of resilience, persistence, and possibility. Beautifully written, her story has something for everyone with profound lessons that are born from the beautiful audacity to prevail and succeed."

—Denice Torres, Healthcare Executive and Board Member, Career/Life Strategist, Host of *Flip the Tortilla* Podcast

"*I Can, I Will & I Did* strikes a chord with its riveting narrative on the power of friendship, resilience, and inner strength. Samina masterfully captures the essence of camaraderie as a beacon during tumultuous times. Her professional odyssey navigating through trials and tribulations epitomizes true resilience—an inspiration for us to face our own hurdles with unwavering determination. Her insights on sustaining emotional grit in the face of adversity are not only poignant, but also deeply enlightening. For anyone looking for a dose of inspiration wrapped in authentic storytelling, this book is a definitive must-read."

—Jim Weiss, Founder & Chairman, Real Chemistry; Executive Advisor, New Mountain Capital

"Brilliantly raw. Brazenly brave. A beautiful account of a trailblazer in her life and career. The vivid descriptions of experiences and encounters at such a young age are palpable and relatable. I laughed and cried. I don't know the people who shaped Samina's life, but somehow, I miss them. I miss Lisa. I miss Doug. I even miss her mom. Because even with the anger Samina felt toward her, I felt sorry for her. When she said that she wondered what it would be like to have a partner who respected her, that almost broke my heart. She was clearly a victim of her life. Samina was a warrior in hers."

—Kalahn Taylor-Clark, PhD, MPH, Faculty at The Johns Hopkins University Carey Business School

"This remarkable book is an inspiring testament to the power of vision and unyielding determination. Raised by immigrant parents who held traditional ideals, the author faced restrictive expectations of what her life should be. Yet, through her clarity of purpose and refusal to conform, she overcame every barrier, reaching the highest levels of success in business, life, and love. Her journey will resonate deeply with anyone who has felt the weight of societal limitations yet dares to dream bigger. This book is an empowering guide for anyone ready to defy the odds and carve their own path to greatness."

—**Kishane Davis, Board Member and VP, Strategy and Partnership Engagement at Momentum and Value for People of Color**

I Can,
I Will
& I Did

Lessons on Life, Love, and Leadership

Samina Bari

WITH MICHELINE AUGER

Black River Publishing
Sheridan, WY

Disclaimer: This book is a memoir. I have tried to recreate events, locales, and conversations from my memories of them. In order to maintain anonymity, in some instances I have changed the names of individuals and places, and some identifying characteristics or details, such as physical properties, occupations, and places of residence.

No memory is perfect, and I respect the fact that each of us has a different perspective about or version of any given event. Nothing in this book is meant to be a criticism or wholesale commentary on individuals, businesses, organizations, or religions. The publishing and marketing of *I Can, I Will & I Did* is not intended to hurt or defame anyone in my personal or professional community. What follows in this book are my memories, impressions, and learnings from formative life events that shaped who I am today.

Published by Black River Publishing
Sheridan, WY

Copyright © 2025 by Samina Bari
www.saminabari.com

First edition 2025

Cover and book design by Sheila Parr
Cover image © iStockphoto / OLENA MATSEPLIUK

Back cover photo credit: Marc Tousignant

Hardcover: 979-8-9919040-0-1
Paperback: 979-8-9919040-1-8
Ebook: 979-8-9919040-2-5
Library of Congress Control Number: 2024924813

Printed in the United States of America

To my father, who always believed in me;
to Lisa, who helped me believe in myself; and
to Doug, whose love enabled me to thrive and
soar in a life of which I had always dreamt.

PREFACE

IF YOU PICKED UP this book thinking that it was about how a brown-skinned, first-generation American overcame racism and sexism to achieve success, you would be wrong. In fact, white men were some of my biggest allies, supporters, and mentors. Sexism, if you want to call it that, came from other women who were my superiors. Call it internalized misogyny or structural patriarchy or both. It came from a culture where women competed for too few roles at the top. Echoing Madeleine Albright's words, "There is a special place in hell for women who don't help other women," I have mentored other women, and it is in that spirit that I write this book.

What do you do when you face a person or culture that wants to destroy you or take away the very essence of who you are? How do you survive?

For me, that person was my mother.

It's not to say that I've never received a racist comment or experienced ignorant behavior based on the color of my skin. I have. And it's not to say that I've never received inappropriate comments from male clients. I have. I can't imagine a woman who hasn't. Yet the biggest hurdle was not from strangers but from my mother, anchored in her unyielding cultural and religious beliefs about how I should act as a girl and a woman. Beliefs that she grew up with and refused to examine or part with. Beliefs that resulted in more than one assault on me when I was a girl by "pious" men within her culture and religion. Beliefs that caused her to look the other way when I needed her most. Beliefs that caused me so much stress that it threatened my mental health.

This kind of abuse, ignorance, and intolerance is not exclusive to any one culture or religion. It's found worldwide and often much closer to home. Yet these attitudes do not define any culture or religion in its entirety. My father, sharing the same religion and culture as my mother, took pride in me, a sentiment that only grew as I matured. When I was growing up, he was not the most emotional or demonstrative man, and work and helping others became his escape.

I learned to escape, as well. First into school and dreaming about the future and then, as an adult, into work and creating the life I always wanted. Every step I took along the way, my mother tried to tear me down. It started at a very young age and continued until the day she died. I drowned her out as much as I could by listening to my heart and using my anger at her to fuel me. Every success was a rebuttal against her doubts.

This book is about not letting anyone stop you from creating the life of your dreams. It's about how to transform pain into strength and creating the love that will sustain you when nothing else can.

PART ONE

The Wrong Kind
of Daughter

CHAPTER ONE

MY MOUTH WAS ON fire. Soon the fire spread slowly down my throat into my belly, threatening to consume me. It was a feeling I would become familiar with. It had the power to destroy me or make me stronger. I chose the latter. And I hope you do, too. Most girls and young women will face oppression of some kind. Girls and young women will confront a culture that wants them to be a certain way. That wants to tell them how to live, how to dress, how to talk, what choices to make and for whom. My story is a story about *not* letting that happen. My story is a story about honoring who you are and creating a life that is uniquely yours even when the people who are entrusted with your care seem determined to do the opposite. If you have a fire in your belly, let it be your fuel. Trust who you are, what you want, and where you want to go, and don't let anyone stop you. Let the fire fuel you.

The first fire that I remember was when I was three years old. My father had just put a green chili pepper into my mouth. Given that he was born and raised in Pakistan, he loved spicy food and wanted me to love it, too. I didn't. Tears streamed down my face as I howled. My mouth burned from the heat. My East Indian mother grabbed the sugar bowl and started shoving spoonfuls of sugar into my mouth. It didn't work.

There's a saying that girls are made of sugar and spice and everything nice. I'd say that girls are made up of the same things that boys are made up of; it's culture that tells them otherwise. In my case, I was the son my father never had and the daughter my mother didn't want. Not to say that she didn't want a daughter, but she wanted a compliant one. She wanted a daughter who would make her look good. She wanted a daughter like the daughters of the other Muslim parents in our small but growing community in Staten Island in the early 1970s. I wasn't the kind of daughter she wanted.

This isn't to say that non-Muslim girls didn't face similar pressures. When I was young, it was a common expectation that girls should grow up to be wives and mothers—that girls should be "everything nice," which often means pleasing and obedient. If a white girl wanted to be a success in business or sports, for example, she could find one or two role models— if she looked hard enough. Maybe not as many as there are now, but they were there. That wasn't really the case if you were a young Muslim American girl, like me.

When I was growing up, I didn't know any Muslim girls who felt the way that I felt. The Muslim girls I knew were compliant. They covered themselves, talked quietly amongst themselves, and were forbidden to do most of the things the boys were allowed to do. They were, essentially, second-class citizens, just like their mothers.

My role models, at the time, if I had any, were the white men I saw on the nightly news, men like Walter Cronkite or the local New York news anchor Chuck Scarborough. If there were any successful Indian/Pakistani women, I didn't know of them, and my mother would have thought them to be unfit role models. In fact, the word Islam means "to submit" and that's exactly what my mother wanted me to do—just as she had done.

My mother grew up in Hyderabad, India. Her family was descended from the well-known 18th-century king, Tipu Sultan, celebrated as an unrelenting freedom fighter who had fought against the British East India Company as it sought to expand its control and domination over Southern India and its people, trade, and natural wealth and resources. His strength on the battlefield earned him the nickname the Tiger of Mysore.

Known as a devout Muslim, he was tolerant of the Hindu religion practiced by a majority of his subjects. His priority was creating and maintaining an independent and technologically advanced city, and, to that end, he created advantageous partnerships with the French against British control.

When I was growing up, I remember hearing that my family owned an original correspondence between my ancestor, the King, and Napoleon Bonaparte, with whom he was seeking an alliance against their mutual enemy, the British. However, the year after that correspondence, Tipu Sultan was killed in battle, and the British stripped his family of all their wealth as punishment. Yet that poverty did not touch my mother. Her father sat on the highest court of India (similar to the U.S. Supreme Court), so she grew up immersed in the wealth and privilege that her father's status dictated.

Their luxurious family home, called Kamal Villa, included a staff of servants and drivers, extensive gardens, and priceless heirlooms that can now be found in India's national museums. Though Kamal Villa no longer exists, my mother's portion of the property was later named after her. Given my mother's upbringing and heritage, perhaps it should be no surprise that she thought herself superior to most people, particularly those who were not Muslim or of her social standing, something that endlessly would embarrass my father and infuriate me.

My mother was the youngest of eight children. While her father prized education, he believed that certain professions were more acceptable than others and wanted each of his children to choose a different one as a career. By the time it was my mother's turn, her father deemed that the only "acceptable" profession remaining was home economics since her older sister had already chosen psychology (which was her first choice). After she received her advanced degree and was "marriageable," her father became ill and, as was expected of the last remaining daughter still living at home, she nursed him until his death. She found herself in her late 20s still unmarried, which, in India in the 1960s, was considered close to spinsterhood. Enter my father.

A man of few words and even fewer expressed emotions, my father grew up in modest means that were closer to poverty than the wealth my mother knew. Perhaps this is why he worked so hard throughout his life to help people who had so little. Born in Azamgarh, India, and raised in the bustling city of Karachi, he was a young teenager when the British finally relinquished their brutal control of India and, in the process, partitioned the country into two, thereby creating Pakistan, which is where my father and his family then found themselves.

It has been said that, during their rule, the British weaponized religion to divide the Indian population against their own interests, separating Hindus, who were in the majority, from Muslims and other religions. With the partition in place, thereby dividing India along religious lines, the British made their rapid exit while the subcontinent exploded in sectarian violence, displacing fifteen million people, and killing more than one million, with an estimated 75,000 women raped and mutilated. This was the reality of living in the post-colonial South Asian world. My father was only sixteen at the time. He had lost his mother four years earlier.

Today, generational and historical trauma are concepts that people are only beginning to talk about. When my father was growing up, trauma was characterized as physical, less so as psychological. Did my parents experience the effects of generational or historical trauma growing up? Are any of us immune to the effects of the past?

My father never spoke about what it was like to live during this time. Nor did he speak about his mother dying, leaving him and his seven brothers in the care of their father. Nor did he talk much about his father remarrying a few years later, adding two half-sisters and a brother into the mix. What I do know is that, twelve years later, when he came to America for a medical internship at the Harlem Hospital in Manhattan, he was looking for a better life. A life away from the cycle of politics and poverty. A life that could offer opportunities to create a better world. He arrived in New York with only one suitcase and a very big dream for the future. If still waters run deep, as the saying goes, this was the case with my father.

My father arrived in America in 1959, the same year that Martin Luther King Jr. made a speech at the Lincoln

Memorial advocating for the integration of schools. Even though the Civil Rights Movement was in full swing, People of Color (or POC) was not a common term as it is now. You were either Black (but not with a capital B) or white, and, in many ways, it was a black-and-white world.

My father, as an Indian-now-Pakistani, was "other" with a capital O. As a child in India, he was part of the Muslim minority. In America, he was just different. His skin color was different. His name was different, and the way he talked was different. Because of this, both patients and doctors, regardless of skin color, treated him differently. Regardless, he immersed himself in his work. The blessing and the curse of medical residencies is that every waking hour is spent at the hospital, and it can be grueling, or a dream come true—or both.

After he completed his internship in Harlem, he went to Staten Island, New York, for a residency. He would return seven years later, after residencies in the Bronx and Halifax, Nova Scotia, and a stint as chief resident in cardiology in Newark, New Jersey. My father had found a home in medicine and a passion for his patients. That was when he truly came alive. In fact, the man I experienced at home was very different from the man patients experienced at the hospital or in his office. It was as if being at work was his escape, just as being at school would soon become mine.

CHAPTER TWO

IT WAS 1966. ANTI-VIETNAM protests were erupting throughout the U.S., Bob Dylan's *Blonde on Blonde* album dropped, and the National Organization for Women was founded in Washington D.C. My father was thirty-five, working as a doctor in a successful private practice, and living in an apartment on Staten Island. It was time to get married.

Luckily, the one person he knew when he arrived in the U.S. was his closest friend, who lived in Manhattan and was married to my mother's older sister, an adolescent psychiatrist. Arranged marriages were to Muslims what swiping right is to today's online dating world, but these two had a "love" marriage.

The conversation between my father and his friend went something like this, "Why don't you marry my wife's sister?" The fact that he hadn't met her was not an issue or even that unusual. It was more important that, on paper at least, they were a good match, and in that regard, they were definitely a good match. He was a doctor, and she came from a good family. My mother's sister wrote my mother a letter and, less than a year later, my father flew to Hyderabad, India, to marry his wife—sight unseen.

After the wedding, my father returned to Staten Island, and my mother followed shortly thereafter, leaving behind her mother and all that she had ever known. She traveled with large metal steamer trunks, packed full of silk saris, family heirlooms, solid silver, and expensive jewelry. This was her dowry. A year later, she would give birth to me.

~

If I came into the world screaming, as many babies do, I wouldn't know. There are no birth or baby stories—in fact, there weren't many stories told at all. The house I grew up in was a quiet one. Oppressively silent is another way to put it. Having a hot pepper put in my mouth would be the first scream I would remember. The rest were internal. Learning how to cope with this would become an ongoing endeavor.

It is true that some people should never have children. My mother was probably one of them. My earliest memory of her (besides spooning sugar into my mouth) was of her in her nightgown, usually lying in bed. She was a light sleeper and suffered from insomnia and, perhaps if it were today, she would have been diagnosed with some form of depression. Fortunately, I was put into preschool at a Montessori on Todt Hill, close to our apartment on Lincoln Avenue. It was during preschool that English was established as my primary language, instead of my parents' native language, Urdu. This was my father's preference, based on the discrimination he faced when he arrived in the United States and his desire for me to truly assimilate without any barriers. This was to the dismay of my mother, who insisted on speaking to me in their native Urdu, to which I would respond in English. My father would speak to me in English but speak to my mother in Urdu. This became the pattern of our lives.

My other keepsake from that early preschool experience is a scar on my arm from being accidentally burned by my preschool teacher's cigarette. In the late 1960s and early 1970s, everybody smoked—even teachers on the playground with children under their charge—which is how it happened. I ran by her as she was flicking the ash off her cigarette, and a preschool memory was born.

My father also smoked, both in the house and the car. This was when cars came equipped with a cigarette lighter and ashtray, a bench seat in the front, and no seatbelts. It was winter and we were driving to the city in my dad's boat-sized Cadillac to visit my aunt and uncle. Anytime we were in the car, my dad would have the AM radio tuned to 1010WINS, whose tagline was "all news, all the time." Clouds of cigarette smoke filled the air, and soon I started coughing. "Stop coughing!" yelled my father. It was almost comedic.

"I can't breathe!" I sputtered. My dad quickly rolled down the windows, and the frigid air rushed in from outside. Relief. It wouldn't be until the mid-'80s that the risks of exposure to secondhand smoke were known.

I hated his smoking. When I was a little older, maybe a pre-teen or tween, I went to the mall and bought him a skull and crossbones ashtray for his birthday, and, when that subtle hint didn't work, I threw his cigarettes in the trash. He was not amused. It wasn't until I was a teenager and he went on a religious pilgrimage that he quit cold turkey. It was like he just flipped a switch. It amazes me to this day that he could quit so easily.

My grandmother also liked tobacco, but, in her case, she preferred chewing tobacco. This was not an uncommon habit in both men and women in India. I met her only once when I was three, when she came to visit my mother and brought her very own sterling silver spittoon. She spent most of her time sitting in the living room, staring out the window with a dour expression—her only movement was a slight turn of her head to spit the tobacco sludge from her mouth into the shiny spittoon. If she had any interest in me, it wasn't obvious, and I found her terrifying. Plus, if this was where my mother got her parenting skills, I would be in trouble. Yet my mother loved her deeply, and, when she passed a few years later, I found my mother sobbing in my father's study.

I was grateful that I had school to go to. Like my dad's work was for him, school became my escape from the silence and solitude at home. My parents enrolled me in St. Clotilde's Academy, a small private K–12 Catholic school that promised a good education, a heavy dose of discipline, and, importantly, no boys. My mother had gone to Catholic school in India and knew the nuns didn't mess around when it came to instilling obedience by threat or by force. This was particularly true of my first-grade teacher, who didn't appreciate the innate curiosity of children. One day, I raised my hand in religion class and asked a series of questions that started with, "How do you know who really wrote the Bible?"

Exasperated by my unrelenting yet completely logical questions, she told me to come to the front of the class and hold out my hands, which I did. She calmly picked up a wooden ruler and, with a good amount of force, whacked my knuckles with it. It hurt. Badly. But she still hadn't answered my questions. This incident did nothing to squelch my innate thirst for facts and evidence over accepting something on blind faith alone, and I would find out that this type of behavior wasn't relegated to Catholic school alone.

Blind faith seems to go hand in hand with unquestioning obedience. One of my earliest and most formative memories happened during Sunday school at the mosque. I was wearing a dress, typical for the little girl that I was. I noticed, however, that the other children were dressed traditionally with their heads covered. Later, the imam made a special visit to my home to tell my father that I wasn't dressed appropriately, and by appropriately he meant modestly. I was only four years old. Though my father was a devout Muslim, he responded angrily.

"It shouldn't matter what she is wearing," he declared in one of the only times I have ever heard him raise his voice. "It should only matter that her intention is to learn. It should only matter what is in her heart." I never attended Sunday school again, and that was the end of any formal Islamic education.

Nonetheless, during the week, I attended Catholic school, and along with that came the weekly mass, which I didn't participate in since I hadn't been baptized and was, after all, a Muslim, technically speaking. During one mass, that all changed, and I feared that I had accidentally converted to Catholicism. Normally I would stand back while the eighth graders shepherded the rest of the first graders into the chapel for communion. This time, an overzealous eighth grader noticed and grabbed my hand.

Ignoring my pleas, she forced me in line to accept Communion. Since I knew the ritual, I obediently knelt, opened my mouth to accept the wafer, and then took a sip from the chalice. I even repeated, "The body and blood of Christ, Amen." Then, I became hysterical. Had I just eaten the body of Christ? Was I now Catholic? My parents were going to kill me.

"Have you been baptized?!" asked the nuns, mortified and on the verge of panic. In the small world of a Staten Island parochial school in the '70s, the nuns knew nothing of other cultures and traditions—much less Islam.

When my father came, as he always did, to pick me up, the nuns quietly told him what had happened. They apologized, assuring him it would never happen again. Meanwhile, I sat in the car, paralyzed with fear. My father got in, lit a cigarette, and turned on the radio. It was the nightly news: A snowstorm was coming, the stock market took another hit, and Samina Bari converted to Catholicism.

Tears streamed down my face. "I'm so sorry," I cried.

"No, no," my father said, gently. "You're only six years old. You didn't do anything wrong." I was so relieved.

Although my parents were devout Muslims, we did celebrate Christmas. It started when I was four years old, and we had just moved to our new home. My dad refused to buy a Christmas tree, but he wasn't against putting a plastic Santa Claus on the fireplace mantel. He also wasn't against buying a boatload of presents, which he purchased at the local mall since my mother didn't drive.

Throughout my life, whenever I received a present, I knew my father had chosen it, even though the card would be signed "Love, Mom and Dad." Even on Valentine's Day, all the way up to adulthood, I would receive a heart-shaped box of chocolates from "Mom and Dad."

Shortly after that first Christmas in our new house, we woke to our first snow in our new neighborhood. My father went outside and stood in our driveway, gazing at the blanketed white world in wonder and appreciation. He felt proud of his new home in this newly developing upper-middle-class neighborhood. He felt proud that he could provide for his family and contribute to the community, and, most of all, he was proud to be an American citizen. During his revelry, the neighbors across the street, who were friends with the neighbors on each side of us, saw my father and spread the word throughout the neighborhood that we were different. Apparently, you're not supposed to stand in front of your house in the middle of a snowstorm in awe—especially if you have brown skin and come from a country no one's heard of. From then on, we were looked at as outsiders, and their children, hearing their parents, took on the same attitude. Over time, it only got worse.

One afternoon, I was with the neighborhood kids when they took out a pack of cigarettes and started smoking behind a neighbor's car. I was shocked. Kids aren't supposed to smoke. I told my parents because I thought that was what you were supposed to do when you were raised to know the difference between right and wrong. My father, concerned, walked over to the neighbor's house and told the parents, thinking that they would want to know. He thought wrong.

"Oh no, not our children," they responded. "Our children are angels." Then they slammed the door in his face.

From then on, I couldn't go outside and play without being harassed and bullied, so my home became a prison.

I would stay inside after school and on weekends and stare out the window at the other kids playing. If I went outside to catch fireflies, which I loved to do, the neighborhood kids would stop what they were doing and call me names and ridicule my parents. It became their favorite pastime.

If this had been all that happened, it would have been tolerable, but it wasn't. Not everyone knows their neighbors, much less gets along with them, but this was just the beginning of what would become over ten years of ostracism and harassment.

One evening during this time, our doorbell rang. My father got up from the dinner table to answer it. There, on the doorstep, was a pile of dog feces. Someone had put it there and lit it on fire. I'll never forget watching my father clean it up without saying a word. Another time, my father's car was broken into while it was parked in our driveway. The kids, now a little older, snickered at him from across the street.

"Call the police!" my mother would say, but my dad feared that it would invite retaliation. Things were bad enough as it was. If my parents needed a permit or an inspection to do any work on the house, the ringleader across the street would use his connections in the buildings department to reject or delay the permits, and what should have been simple became anything but. When that same neighbor put a dumpster in front of his house during a remodel, everyone in the neighborhood would use it, but when my mother tried to, he yelled at her and forced her away.

My mother had already earned herself a bit of a reputation. Whenever she needed someone to work on the house, she'd treat them like a second-class citizen. If they wanted a glass of water, they'd have to drink from the hose. If they needed to use the bathroom, she'd tell them to go into the woods. She didn't believe in tipping and always haggled about even reasonable prices. Even our housekeeper of more than twenty years couldn't drink out of our glasses. Instead, my mother gave her a grape jelly jar to use. That became her assigned glass.

Was this the reason we were bullied? Not entirely. We were bullied because we were "different." This small-mindedness became one of the reasons "I have to get out of here" became the reoccurring thought in my head. I didn't know where I would go, but I knew it would be far away from that neighborhood and community, and far away from a home that felt more like a prison.

CHAPTER THREE

IF MY MOTHER HAD a passion, it was for criticizing me, and it started early. When I came home from school with a 98% on a test, she'd say, "Where is the other 2%? You are careless." I was a six-year-old child. If I was in the kitchen helping her wash a dish, she'd say I wasn't washing it correctly. I wasn't using hot enough water. I didn't put it in the dish rack correctly. If I made tea, she'd say that I had steeped it too long or not long enough. She'd say I didn't use enough milk, or I used too much milk. It was either too hot or not hot enough. Was she treated this way by her mother growing up? I didn't know, because we never talked about that or anything else, and, when I was little, I didn't care. All I knew was that I couldn't stand it.

My mother was an incredible cook. I still crave her haleem, nihari and biryani. I never learned those recipes because it was so uncomfortable to be with her long enough for her to teach me. Instead, I learned to stay away from the kitchen and from her as much as possible.

Fortunately, since she stayed in bed for most of the day,

I didn't have to see her in the mornings before school. From kindergarten through elementary school, my dad would wake me up and I would get myself dressed in my school uniform that I had laid out the night before. Then, I'd go meet my dad downstairs where he'd sit, drinking his Sanka instant coffee, smoking his cigarette, and reading the paper. I would find the bowl and spoon that my mother had left on the counter the night before, placed next to the cereal boxes. My father and I wouldn't talk. It would just be silent. When it was time, he'd drive me to school in his smoke-filled car tuned to the "All News, All the Time" radio station that became one of the soundtracks of my childhood.

After school, the school bus would drop me off four blocks from our house. My mother, by then, would have managed to get out of bed and out of her nightgown so she could pick me up. We'd walk down the street, crossing it at one point to avoid the German shepherd that she was afraid of, and then reach our house, ignoring any neighbors that might be throwing looks our way, and on into the kitchen, where I'd grab a snack and do my homework. That was the daily ritual.

Dinner was also quiet—painfully quiet. There is an old *Saturday Night Live* skit where a family sits at a dinner table together and all you hear is the cutlery against the plates as they uncomfortably have nothing to say to each other. This was how it was at my house. To avoid this, I started chattering about anything and everything I could think of—some of it was pure nonsense. This would not result in any form of a conversation. It was sort of like having the radio on in the car—except it was me talking to fill the silence until it was time for me to leave the table.

After dinner, I would find my father sitting at his desk in his study watching the evening news. We called it the "blue room." When I was little, I'd crawl up on his lap and we'd watch Walter Cronkite delivering the news in a way that felt calmly reassuring. Sitting with my father was my main source of affection, and I relished it. We were not a touchy-feely family. There were no tickle-fights or hugs. I would watch *Leave It to Beaver* and other family shows on TV and notice the parents being affectionate with each other and their children. When I was in kindergarten, I begged my parents to kiss each other. When my dad finally gave in and awkwardly leaned over to force a peck on my mother's cheek, it was anything but affectionate.

After the dishes were done, my mother would join us, sitting in her chair. This was our family time. The TV was on, with four broadcast channels to choose from (no streaming or cable), and we were all together. We would watch comedies like *The Carol Burnett Show*, *I Love Lucy*, or, surprisingly, *Benny Hill*. If there was laughter in the house, it was the laughter from the studio audiences of these shows (although my dad would occasionally laugh at Ricky Ricardo's reaction to Lucy and, of course, at Benny Hill's ridiculous and wildly suggestive antics). The TV was a welcome break from the deadening silence.

By the time I was eight, I'd forgo this family time and escape to my bedroom to listen to music quietly on my clock radio. My bedroom had been decorated by Emma, an interior designer my mother had become friends with. Emma was twenty years older than my mother, which was appealing since my mother couldn't relate to Western women her age or younger.

Emma had style with a capital S, sporting a black bouffant hairdo and wearing gradient sunglasses and loud prints. It was fitting for a woman of a certain age, but she lacked an appreciation for the tastes of a little girl. I found myself surrounded by three walls painted a light Pepto-Bismol pink, with the fourth wallpapered in a faint white polka-dotted pattern against a light green background. To make matters worse, the room was carpeted in bright red to match the cover on the trundle bed, which was upholstered in red pleather and finished with white piping. The bed could be pulled apart to create a sofa on one side of the room with the remaining twin on the other.

In the evenings, I would lie on my bed and stare at the polka dots trying to ignore the garishness of the room. In the background, my AM/FM clock radio would softly play "You Light Up My Life," sung by a melancholy-sounding Debby Boone. I listened to her sing about loneliness, about dreams buried deep inside, and about being saved from the darkness of her own life. I could relate to that loneliness. I also wanted to be saved, but I was starting to suspect that the only one who would save me would be me. I would dream about my future life where I would meet and marry my handsome prince with green eyes and dimples, and we would have adorable children together. He and my future life would be the opposite of what my parents would expect of me, and together we'd live a life of happiness and contentment—feelings that were painfully missing in my life.

My mother would come alive around 11 p.m. when the telephone rates were cheaper. She'd abandon the TV and my father's smoke-filled study and commandeer the rotary phone in her bedroom. The room would fill with gossip and bickering, which was the love language of choice when it came to her sisters, brothers, cousins, and favorite brothers-in-law. These were probably her closest, most loving relationships. If she was unhappy or needed help with my father, she'd confide in her brother-in-law, my father's best friend, who viewed her as a little sister. Later, when she wanted to get a job as a librarian, she would ask him to advocate on her behalf to my father since he strictly forbade the idea of her working. It was against Islamic tradition and, in his eyes, a particular embarrassment since he earned more than enough money to support the family. Certainly, in the 1970s, he wasn't the only husband to think this way—Muslim or not.

Instead, he suggested that she volunteer at the hospital, which is what most of the doctors' wives did, but she considered this beneath her. She wanted to be paid for her time, regardless of the limited experience or skills she had to offer. This arrogance, though real, was also a cover for her lack of confidence. "But I don't speak correctly," she'd say, but she'd refuse to take English language classes. Instead, a palpable sense of inertia settled into the unfulfilled moments of her day, periodically interrupted by brief periods of inspiration that would later be abandoned.

One of those moments of inspiration led her to take a cooking class. Though she was an incredible cook of Indian cuisine, her repertoire of American dishes consisted of dry chicken breasts, gray-looking steaks cooked in the broiler, overboiled frozen vegetables, or basic salads with bottled dressings. When I was very young, she would resort to serving TV dinners on a TV tray, usually on Thursday nights when my dad had his office hours, but learning American cuisine would change all that—or so she (and we) thought.

After class, she'd come home and talk about all the great recipes that she was making in class and would make for us at home, but they never materialized. What did materialize was a new friendship with a woman in class who seemed to know everyone on Staten Island. When my dad and I learned her name, it became clear that my mother's new friend came from a family that was more than a little "connected"—meaning notorious. It wasn't *The Sopranos* but could have been close. My mother didn't have a clue. She was so naive. The friendship didn't last, but her limited cooking skills did.

Another one of her short-lived dreams took her to NYC for electrolysis classes. She would return home excited to start her own business, which she wanted to run out of our house and on her own terms, but she didn't want the women from her Muslim community to know about it. They wouldn't approve. Once she realized how much money and work it would entail, that plan, like all the others, would soon come to an end and the inertia would return.

I don't know if my house felt as lonely to my parents as it did to me, but I suspect it might have, as there was never a shortage of places to be on the weekends and some weeknights. My father, who was one of the first Pakistanis on Staten Island (and the first Pakistani physician), was an integral part of building what would become a growing and vibrant Muslim community. Proud to be an American citizen, he helped other Muslim immigrants become engaged citizens through his work with the American Muslim Alliance, which he founded, as well as the local mosque, where he was a charter member. He would set up meetings between the Pakistani community and the Staten Island borough president and other city officials so that the community could assimilate successfully. Because of my father's work, we were embraced and welcomed here, as well as within the larger Muslim communities of New Jersey and Queens.

Within this community, my mother was her most comfortable and most animated. Outside of it, she would "forget" people's names and remain silent with a fake smile plastered on her face. She preferred to be called "Mrs. Bari," rather than by her first name, even by the parents of my lifelong friends or "the girls" who worked in my father's office practice for forty years.

This cold aloofness softened when she attended the many events within the Muslim community, which were held at the mosque, in community halls, or private homes on Staten Island, New Jersey, or Queens. When we arrived, the men would be with the men, the boys with the boys, and the girls and women were expected to do the same. There was no mixing between the genders. This segregation felt ridiculous to me. I wanted to be with the men and the boys, who were talking, laughing, and having more fun than the women or girls.

The boys could run around and play and wear short-sleeved shirts and pants, but the girls were expected to sit quietly and keep their heads, arms, and legs covered. The men would talk about world events and politics, while the women would discuss domestic topics or gossip. I hated it. When food was served, the women and girls were expected to eat last, after serving the men and boys. When I'd question my mother about this, she'd just answer, "This is what we do." That was her answer to everything. If I asked her to discuss or explain the Qur'an to me, she couldn't, even though she was an educated woman. Tradition and blind faith were enough for her.

This would be one of the many ongoing conflicts in our relationship. It's not that I wasn't a compliant or well-behaved child. I just refused to be or do anything on blind faith, so if my mother (like the nuns in school) couldn't offer fact-based explanations for what she said or thought, then I would remain true to my rational self. The belief that women and girls needed to dress modestly to not tempt men struck me as absurd, so I refused to dress traditionally, wearing long pants and long-sleeved shirts instead. My mother carried a scarf in her purse for me so that I could cover my head when we'd arrive someplace, but I'd take it off as soon as I could. The other girls my age who dressed and acted the way that was expected of them seemed like sheep to me. I couldn't relate. I was the black sheep—at least in my mother's eyes and in the eyes of the Muslim community.

My mother was all or nothing: If you didn't do it all, you weren't good enough. And because I refused to do it all, I was never good enough. This was the difference between my mother and my father. My father was able to embrace Western culture while still honoring his religion and tradition. When we went to the restaurant at the Holiday Inn to celebrate one of their wedding anniversaries, my father ordered a glass of wine and encouraged my mother to do the same, but she refused.

"No alcohol will ever touch my lips," she'd say. "It's forbidden."

This rigid attitude of intolerance was why school became such an escape for me. It was the one place I felt safe and free to be me—until, one day, that changed, too.

CHAPTER FOUR

MUCH TO MY MOTHER'S dismay, I felt more of an affinity with the girls at the St. Clotilde's Academy than I ever did with the Muslim girls in my parents' community. Most of the girls were Catholic, and a good majority were Italian or Irish or both. It wasn't until fourth grade that a Jewish girl joined the school, which seemed to cause a greater stir than my presence.

"Why is a Jewish girl going to a Catholic school?" the girls would whisper—never mind that I was Muslim. I think it was because they knew what Jewish was, or at least had heard of it, but didn't really understand what a Muslim was, so they ignored it. For all intents and purposes, I was one of them, and I liked that. I liked feeling a part of this community of girls, and it didn't feel like I had to change who I was to do so. I did, though, try to change my name.

It was in first grade that I noticed that all the girls had middle names and I didn't. I felt left out. When I asked my dad about it, he said, "Don't worry. You can use mine." This seemed fitting since he always bragged that he was the one who named me, and he never failed to tell people that my name, Samina, meant precious. Now I had a middle name too and I couldn't wait to use it. The next day, we had a test and on it, I wrote Samina Mohammed Bari. It looked great, but when the teacher saw it, she became confused.

"Is this your name?" she asked. "Because if this is your name, we need to update your records."

The next morning when my father was dropping me off, she asked him about it. He just laughed. That was the end of my middle name. When it came down to it, I realized that I didn't need it to feel like I belonged with the other girls.

In the first few years of grade school, my friendships were, in some way, determined by the person's proximity to our house or my father's office. One friend, Beth, lived close to my dad's office, so I could go there after school. I also got to know her neighborhood friends, who were nothing like the bullies in mine. Beth and I were born a day apart at the hospital where my dad worked, and our mothers shared the same room, so we had a special relationship. Ana, who joined the school in third grade, lived down the street from my house, so I would often go there to do my homework. Her parents were both doctors, and her mother knew my dad from the hospital. This was one of the first times that I saw parents helping their kids with their schoolwork, and sometimes they would help me as well.

This wasn't the case at my home. My mother couldn't help me, and the one time my dad tried to help me with a fourth-grade math assignment, he lost his temper, so that was the end of that. Ana and I became close friends for some time, but then her mother, who could be incredibly harsh, decided that she wanted Ana to associate with only the "very best of people." She was sent to a private high school in New Jersey, and our friendship ended.

For most of my school years, my closest friends were Lisa and Mary. I can't remember a particular moment when these friendships began, because it feels like I've known them for as long as I can remember. Lisa and I started in kindergarten together, and Mary joined in the first grade. We were always in the same classes except when Mary would go to her advanced math classes. No matter how hard I studied, I'd get B's, but Mary would get A's without much effort. Oftentimes, I would go to her house to do homework, and this was another time when I saw how other kids' parents would help them with their homework. When it came to Lisa and Mary, their parents became parental figures for me as well, and, in high school, Lisa's mom would, in many ways, replace mine altogether.

Lisa was Italian, and everyone thought we were sisters, which I loved. She had dark hair and skin, and thick eyebrows like me. Mary was Irish and Italian, and her family seemed like the quintessential "normal" American family. Her mom was a nurse, and her dad was an executive. They both prioritized education. Both Mary and her older brother ended up becoming doctors as well as marrying doctors.

Lisa's parents were younger than the other parents, and, when Lisa and I became close in high school, you could always find me at their house. I had grown up with her mother, Fran, who was always at our school volunteering for some event or dressing up as a witch at our school Halloween party. Her dad was a tall, large, intimidating-looking man with a dark beard and mustache and, even though I was initially afraid of him, he too would become a father figure, even though my parents were wary of them. They weren't like Mary's parents, meaning "white collar." Instead, they owned several local businesses, and my mother thought this was less than respectable given her class-based attitude. Regardless of what she thought, their home would become my home, and every formative experience I had throughout adolescence and adulthood would be shared with Lisa. Ultimately, these friendships nurtured my soul and fulfilled my emotional needs in a way that my parents could not.

~

During the summer break, I couldn't escape to school. Instead, we would drive down to Sumter, South Carolina, to visit my mother's other sister, my uncle, and their two sons. I would spend most of my time in the local library making my way through the thirty books on my school's summer reading list. My uncle, who was a professor, would spend time with me discussing what I was reading, and these became some of my favorite moments.

When not at the library, I loved going to Myrtle Beach, which, at the time, was nothing like the tourist attraction it became after the development boom of the 1990s. Going to the beach or a friend's pool was particularly exciting because, at home with my parents, I was stuck inside watching the neighborhood kids playing in their backyard pools. My parents didn't value outdoor activities, and the bullying didn't help. For those reasons, I didn't learn how to swim or ride a bike until I was an adult.

But during these summers, I'd play for hours in the shallow end of the pool, even if my mother didn't like it when my skin would get dark. She considered light skin beautiful and darker skin indicative of a lower class. Later, in high school, Lisa and I would spend hours floating on a raft in her pool trying to get a tan. We didn't mind being dark.

Almost all of my formative experiences in life came from outside my family. It was because of my aunts and uncles that I got to do these things, or because of my friends at school that I would see different ways of being a family. Even seemingly small things, like loving and playing with a dog as a pet versus an animal to be afraid of was new to me. I grew because of my summers away, and my friends and I continued to look for people and experiences that would help me grow outside of the narrow confines of my home and family.

Apart from these summers, vacations consisted of going to the Islamic Medical Association of North America annual meetings, which were, of course, events that I dreaded. They were held inside convention centers with planned (a.k.a. mandatory) bus tour excursions, and, again, I was required to dress in long pants and long-sleeved shirts.

The first IMA meeting I went to was held at Disney World in Florida. It was January and it snowed—a very rare occasion in Florida. I was embarrassed to be a part of this large group of Muslim women and children who didn't speak English in public, dressed differently, and were constantly stared at. I didn't want to be associated with them. Throughout all subsequent meetings, we would participate in the bus excursions and I would feel the same sense of dread and embarrassment. I couldn't wait until I was old enough to avoid coming to these events, yet even when I was in college, my dad asked me to go with him because the event was in Costa del Sol in Malaga, Spain.

"If I go, I'm going to go to the beach and I'm going to wear a bikini," I warned him. He agreed.

It ended up being the biggest disaster—not for me but for the thousands of Muslims who soon discovered that the beaches in Spain were topless. Little Muslim boys would hang over the balconies gawking at the women. I'll never forget seeing my father walk down the beach in his three-piece suit looking for us. His face was beet red as he tried not to look anywhere. I couldn't help but laugh, not at my father, but at this community that had felt so restrictive and punishing when I was growing up. But even then, I would come up with strategies to escape.

CHAPTER FIVE

AT ELEVEN YEARS OLD, I was one of the first girls in my class to develop breasts. Thank goodness I went to an all-girls school. My mother preferred to be in denial and refused to buy me a bra, and these were not the little buds of bigger breasts to come. This was full-on womanhood on a little girl's body. I also had braces, eyeglasses, a slight mustache, and a unibrow. It was not a good look. Instead of a bra, I had to wear an undershirt, which was painful and embarrassing. I begged my aunt to talk to my mother about getting me a bra.

It was not news to either of my aunts that my mother was uncomfortable about this phase of my development. My mother had admitted to her sister a few summers earlier that she was too embarrassed to talk to me about these things. I would have to learn about puberty elsewhere. It turned out I would have to learn from my cousin.

"Do you know about a woman's period?" my cousin asked.

"Of course," I said, not completely understanding. "You

mean like a period of time?" We were hiding underneath the dining room table so that our boy cousins wouldn't find us.

"No," she said, shaking her head. "It's when you start bleeding."

When I finally got my period, I went to my mother and told her. "I'm bleeding," I said.

"Right," she said. "Come with me."

I followed her to the bathroom, where she handed me a very large maxi pad and belt. It might as well have been an adult diaper. My mother considered tampons *haram*, which means forbidden by Islam. Though this was not the case, many, especially of my mother's generation, believed tampons could break the hymen. Instead of this being a bonding moment between mother and daughter, it was just another uncomfortable one—like having to ask my dad to buy me pads at the store since my mother didn't drive.

So when my aunt finally persuaded my mother to buy me a bra, it was my dad who drove us to the department store to buy it. Predictably, instead of buying me the women's bra that had the support that I needed, she picked out a thin teen bra that looked purer and more innocent in her eyes. I still have stretch marks from wearing the wrong-sized bra simply because my mother was uncomfortable with my adolescent body. Everything around womanhood seemed cloaked in her religious shame, as if breasts and periods and simply being female were wrong and should therefore be hidden or ignored. When it came time for me to shave my legs, the same was true. My hair was dark, and it was growing in on my legs quite visibly. Again, I went to my aunt and begged her to talk to my mother about letting me shave my legs. If

I asked my mother for anything, she'd just refuse. After my aunt talked to her, she acquiesced.

One of the best things about adolescence and getting my period was that I could use it as an excuse to avoid going to the mosque, since women and girls weren't allowed to attend while they were bleeding. This led me to "fake a period" every chance I got. Fearing that my mother wouldn't believe me, I'd roll up a pad in a disposable bag and toss it in the bathroom trash can as proof. Soon, I used this excuse to get out of any community event I could because, after all, menstruating women were dirty. It was the silver lining of an awkward (at best) and horrifying (at worst) puberty.

Around this same time, my mother decided that I should take piano lessons because her friends' daughters were, so she bought an upright piano "for me." What I needed was a proper bra, not a piano or piano lessons. Luckily, the lessons didn't last long because Sister Sophia, who was also my eighth-grade teacher, told me that to play the piano properly, I needed to cut my long, manicured nails. I wasn't about to do that. The piano would remain unused in my parents' house for the next twenty years. What I needed or wanted didn't matter. My mother just wanted to avoid the fact that I was growing up.

It was around this time that I became tired of the adults in my parents' community asking me what I was going to be when I grew up. These questions had been going on since I was six years old! It was ridiculous. Without waiting for my answer, my parents would invariably state, "She's going to be a doctor." Obviously, they weren't the only parents who said this about their children, and many of their peers' children did, in fact, grow up to become doctors. In my case, the pressure and constant questioning probably had the opposite effect and played a big role in my not becoming a doctor.

If my parents had paid attention, they would have noticed that the more they told me to do something, the less likely I would be to do it. I wasn't trying to be disobedient. I was simply not wired that way, and shaming me wasn't going to change that no matter how hard my mother tried—and tried she did. When her shame became a betrayal, I had no other choice but to emotionally distance myself from her for good.

CHAPTER SIX

MY PARENTS FREQUENTLY HOSTED parties for their community. One evening, when I was helping by serving drinks, my mother scolded me because I had looked a male guest in the eye, smiled, and said, "You're welcome." If the guest had been a woman, there wouldn't have been a problem, but, since it was a man, what I had done was, in her opinion, improper and disrespectful. Instead, I should have known better and kept my eyes focused downward. "Never look a man in the eye," was the credo.

This type of criticism and scrutiny was nothing new, but as I entered puberty it intensified. In addition to what I wore, it also applied to my behavior, and I was given a litany of "don'ts, won'ts, and can'ts." "Don't show a man the bottom of your foot because it's a sign of disrespect," she'd scold. "You will not look a man in the eye," she'd demand. "You can't cross your legs in front of a man," she'd admonish. It never seemed to end. Was she trying to help me? It certainly didn't feel that way, and when I really needed her help, she couldn't, wouldn't, and didn't.

When I was thirteen years old, we were attending a small dinner party at the home of a friend of my mother's (a zany friend whom I wasn't a huge fan of and who led my mother on more than one misadventure). The guests also included a couple I had grown up with and who were like trusted family. My father had witnessed the birth of their firstborn, bestowing the customary blessing, and we had them in our home many times. As the men sat in the living room drinking scotch, the women chatted in the kitchen, and I found myself alone in the bedroom with the husband of the young couple. Suddenly, he pushed me against the wall and kissed me, his tongue penetrating my mouth. Shocked and terrified, I pushed him away and ran out of the room. I didn't say a word to anyone.

For weeks, I lost sleep, struggling to make sense of what had happened, until I finally realized I had to say something. I summoned up the courage to tell my mother, convinced that she would be aghast at his behavior. But it wasn't his behavior that she was aghast at.

"No, no," she said in Urdu. "Absolutely not. What did *you* do?" she accused, as if I had done something to tempt him.

In that moment, something irrevocably broke in our relationship and it would never be the same. It felt like a steel door had slammed shut around my heart. My mother refused to tell my father, and I certainly couldn't. If my mother reacted this way, what would he do? And if she did tell him, what would she say? Would she make it my fault? Would she call me a liar and blame me all over again? In the years following, I put the incident behind me and directed my anger toward my mother, who took this man's side instead of mine and failed to believe me or keep me safe. It wasn't the first time she had betrayed me, but it was the worst, and my heart closed to her, forever.

My parents continued to be close with this family, and, by extension, I had to be as well, even though I would never forget the incident. My father, who would remain unaware of what had occurred when I was only thirteen, considered the husband a close friend, and I was not ready to shatter that. Because of that, this "family friend" would go on to bear witness to my marriage and take an active role at the end of my parents' lives. I focused all my animosity from the event on my mother. It was her job to protect me and she failed.

This is an all-too-common experience for young girls and women, no matter what country or culture they live in: first, to be sexually assaulted (which is what it was) and then to be disbelieved and, even worse, blamed for it—sometimes by the people closest to you. Years before I had my own daughters, I knew I would protect and defend my girls as any mother should.

Unfortunately, this wasn't the last experience of this kind. The following year, we took a trip to Saudi Arabia as part of my parent's pilgrimage to Mecca. Because Islamic law is strictly enforced, I was forced to wear a black abaya, which is a traditional black garment that completely covers the body, along with a black headscarf to cover my hair, and, to be safe, my parents wanted me to wear the abaya over long pants and a long-sleeved shirt.

It was over 100 degrees out, and we were in a taxi without air conditioning. I felt like I was on the verge of heatstroke. Since we were in the cab, my parents allowed me to take off my head covering so I could at least feel the hot breeze from the open windows. When we arrived, I stepped out of the taxi with my parents, when suddenly, I felt something hit my body. I felt it again and spun around to find a group of old and middle-aged men standing across the street hurling rocks at me and yelling at us in Arabic, which neither of my parents understood. I looked at my parents, shocked and confused. We were all panicked.

"Your hair," my dad exclaimed, finally understanding what was happening. "Cover your hair, quickly!"

I grabbed my scarf, and, frantically, put it on. I had simply forgotten and now I was literally being stoned. This wasn't the Middle Ages. This (and far worse) still happens today. I was furious. I didn't even want to be here. I didn't want to be part of this pilgrimage. I didn't want to be a part of any form of ignorance and oppression. From being whacked on the knuckles by a nun who couldn't explain the Bible to being stoned by grown men for "immodesty," I was done with religion. The thought that went through my head was, "fuck this." I counted the days when I could escape back to my friends, studies, and school.

On the last day in Jeddah, my mother and her cousin who lived there took me to an outdoor market where jewelry, textiles, spices, and other souvenirs are sold. Men and women roamed the area, with women fully covered, holding their bags, and men walking with their hands clasped behind their backs. Relieved to be away from the obligatory religious and familial gatherings, I enjoyed a moment of normalcy trying on rings and bracelets. As I was looking into a storefront, I caught a glimpse of a man walking toward me with his hands behind his back. Thinking nothing of it, I turned back to the jewelry. As he passed behind me, he groped me from outside my abaya. Shocked, I turned around and yelled at him. My mother ran over, also shocked, but she, of course, wasn't shocked at the man. She was shocked at me. How dare I yell at a man? How dare I look the man in the eye? How dare I look the police in the eye who were now holding me, forcefully, while yelling at me in Arabic?

"Apologize," pleaded my mother's cousin. I was incredulous. Why should I apologize for what that man did to me?! I didn't do anything wrong. *He* should apologize.

"Apologize or you will go to jail," she said. I looked at my mother for some show of support.

"Say you're sorry!" she yelled at me.

The men laughed. Even though they pretended they couldn't understand English, I could tell they knew exactly what was going on.

Again, I felt that familiar burning inside. My whole body was on fire with outrage. First, I'm stoned for not covering my head, then I'm groped. Then, I'm told to apologize to the man who did it. There wasn't a cell in my body that would allow me to do that.

My mother's cousin turned to the police and, in Arabic, told them that I was sorry. "She's just a silly girl from America," she said. "She doesn't know anything. Please accept our apologies."

Finally, I was released, and we were allowed to leave.

My mother told my dad what happened, but we never spoke of it. What could he do? When rocks were being thrown at me, he didn't say anything to the men who did it. I knew it upset him, but he kept it inside. He grew up in a conservative Muslim family in India and Pakistan, where this behavior was not unusual, but I always sensed a struggle within him about this aspect of the culture.

A few years earlier when we had visited his oldest brother in Pakistan, he said nothing while his 7'2" brother towered over him, berating him for allowing my mother to raise me so poorly and for his failings to enforce my mother's duty for my education and religious upbringing in the marriage. It didn't matter that I was a good student. The offense was that I didn't know the Qur'an or speak Urdu. I was angry at my dad for not defending my mother, who was quietly and subserviently looking at the ground while everyone in the room cringed at the scene. Then I realized my father couldn't do anything. He was trapped too. It wasn't until I followed in my father's footsteps that I began to appreciate the depth of his humanity and caring.

~

"I want to get a job," I told him. We were back in Staten Island, and I was yearning for independence, but, just like with my mother earlier, my dad forbade me from having a paid job.

"You don't need to work," he said. "You are a doctor's daughter. I earn enough." It wasn't even that I wanted the money, I just wanted to get out of the house. I wanted to be free—unlike the life my mother lived.

"You can volunteer at the hospital," he offered, so I did. Little did I know that I would find the first hints of a calling in the very place I was born. It was also where I would see my father at his best and happiest.

As the chief of staff, my father's name was constantly

announced over the loudspeaker. Everyone knew and respected him, and, even more, they adored him. I saw him laughing and joking with the staff at various nurses' stations throughout the hospital. I witnessed him listening empathetically to his patients. This was quite a contrast to the quiet man that I experienced at home. It was almost like he was another person altogether. It was in seeing this that my love and appreciation for him grew. He inspired me. I, too, wanted to help people. I just didn't know how yet.

My father had founded the dementia clinic years earlier and, since it was the early '80s, the Mentally Retarded and Developmentally Disabled, or MRDD, clinic. I remember seeing patients wearing helmets and banging their heads against the wall, and it frightened me. I didn't understand. My father had fought to get the clinic started and funded because, prior to that, these patients had no help and were essentially forgotten.

He did the same with eldercare, founding the first seniors' clinic for people who had, up to then, been overlooked. I watched as he greeted every patient with respect and care and, in return, they showered him with admiration and kindness.

When he noticed that many of the seniors were alone on Thanksgiving, he founded an annual Sunday Thanksgiving Dinner, rallying nurses, doctors, and the hospital CEO himself to help decorate the hospital cafeteria and then serve the seniors a three-course meal. He even raised money to provide transportation, since most of the seniors didn't drive. I spent many years volunteering at these dinners through early adulthood and will never forget the bright smiles and shining eyes of his patients as they took his face in their quivering hands and thanked him.

As a volunteer, I was assigned to serve food to the patients in the dementia ward. I would bring meals to the same woman every day, and every day, she would greet me like it was the first time. Every day, she'd ask my name. Every day, she'd tell me the same story. And, every day, I'd greet her with a smile on my face until one day, I finally broke down, crying. I couldn't do it. I couldn't remain emotionally detached. This upwelling of emotion surprised me because there was so little emotion expressed or seemingly felt in my home. Yet, in a setting like this, I had little control. It all came out. I would have to find my calling elsewhere.

I would find it in the unlikeliest of places doing a task that most people would abhor. It was July 14, 1984, and Union 1199, which represents nonmedical employees at thirty private and nonprofit hospitals, including the hospital where my father worked, went on what would become a historic and groundbreaking strike. It was the longest and largest healthcare walkout to that date, lasting forty-seven days and affecting eighteen thousand patients. I was fifteen years old at the time and called in to help out due to the severe staffing shortage. In no time, I found myself cleaning up the operating rooms after the surgeries. I was in heaven. Who knew that I would love cleaning up what most people would find disgusting? Most people prefer their blood and guts in a horror movie, but I preferred mine in the OR. This is where people are taken apart and put back together again. This is where things get fixed. I wanted to be a part of that— part of making things better. Part of the solution.

The strike was finally resolved with union members getting a 5 percent wage increase and a guarantee of every other weekend off. Things returned to normal, and I thought my

OR days were over until I was lucky enough to be invited to sit in and observe the surgeries. I would stand behind the surgeons and watch everything—from a colectomy (where part or all of a colon is removed) to a cesarean section, to the removal of breast implants. If I was too emotionally attached to handle direct patient care, I was well-equipped, emotionally and otherwise, for the realities of surgery. Is this where I would find my home?

I didn't think so. At the time, there were few women in residency programs, and surgical residency programs were long and grueling. Plus, if I gave in to my parents now and became the doctor they always wanted, the badgering would never stop. First, it would be about becoming a doctor; then it would be about becoming a wife and a mother. Even though I did want those things, I wanted them on my terms.

CHAPTER SEVEN

ENTERING HIGH SCHOOL IS usually a big and exciting transition for a teenager. Not so at St. Clotilde's Academy. It was essentially the same girls and the same school except for one very important thing. I didn't have to take religion classes or participate in Mass anymore. Instead, I would take a study period and dive into my biology or chemistry homework. I didn't want to admit that I enjoyed these subjects because I feared that it meant that my parents were right in their desire that I should study medicine. Instead, I kept my love of science a secret. I also thrived in my AP English and history classes and found a love for journalism and the arts. Growing up watching the news and finding solace in the world of reading had prepared me well. My world and interests were expanding, and I loved it.

The following summer, when my friends went on vacation or hung out at the Jersey Shore, I enrolled myself in summer school geometry class trying to avoid my mother and life at home. It was my first class with boys. Suddenly, I found myself shy and afraid to raise my hand and participate. Still, I was a good student, and, over time, I became more comfortable.

During this time, I decided to see what would happen if I took the Regents Exam early. Students needed to pass the Regents Exam to be awarded a final diploma. Since I wasn't great at taking standardized tests, I thought this would be good practice. Much to my surprise, I passed my "practice" test and was subsequently placed in advanced classes, including math. I hadn't expected this because I underestimated myself—especially when it came to math. It turned out that advanced math was not a problem for me at all.

Volunteering and summer school were my carefully orchestrated attempts to be away from home as much as possible. My friendship with Lisa grew stronger each day, and I spent as much time as possible at her house. Lisa's mom became the mother I had always wanted, and her dad treated me like his own. Their house became the go-to place for hanging out daily and for weekend parties.

There were a lot of firsts there: My first party with boys, my first beer, and my first real kiss all took place at a party at their house. The music was blasting with songs by The Police, Michael Jackson, and Survivor. The house was so packed that kids spilled out onto the lawn. I was, in that moment, the quintessential American teenager and I loved every moment of it. I was Pretty in Pink with very, VERY big hair, teased to its fullest, and sprayed with a ton of Stiff Stuff hairspray. At one point, I was sitting on a boy's lap kissing him when Lisa's dad grabbed me by the scruff of my neck, like a kitty, and pulled me off of him.

"Nope," he said. "You are like a daughter to me. You do not do that."

I wasn't in trouble, and he wasn't mad at me. He was just being protective, and I knew, from that point on, that Lisa's parents would always be there for me, no matter what. There may have been drinking and many more parties to come, but they were the parents that you trusted, the parents you knew that you could go to no matter what, and the parents who were exceedingly responsible. In my eyes, it's the parents who don't show they care or who are overly strict that ultimately fail their parental responsibility.

Lisa was popular and knew tons of kids outside of our school. She seemed to be friends with everyone, and her friends became my friends—particularly a group of boys from St. Vitus High School. We became fast friends, and I trusted them. They would pick us up from school and drive us home. I became close friends with a boy named Ethan who would drive me home from school or stop by my house some nights in his souped-up white pickup truck. Of course, my parents flipped out.

"How do you know these boys?!" they demanded.

"They're my friends," I'd say, nonchalantly.

"How? You go to an all-girls school," they'd counter. "You shouldn't be friends with boys!"

If they were leery of my friendship with Lisa, this didn't help, but, for me, these friends and experiences became another escape from a stifling home into a normal teenage life. No longer did I feel alienated and alone. No longer did I feel like a failure. I was one of the gang, and it felt great. On weekends, we'd pile into Lisa's dad's Porsche and drive up and down Hylan Boulevard doing the very '80s pastime of "cruising." After that got old, we would head to the city or Brooklyn and sneak into the popular dance clubs.

Whatever clubbing clothes I owned would be kept safely at Lisa's house, and that's where we'd get ready to go out, spending no less than two hours on hair and carefully applied makeup. My parents would send Lisa's mom fruit baskets and flowers thanking her for letting me stay over at Lisa's house so often. My mother thought we were studying. If she had only known.

On my 16th birthday, Lisa gave me a charm that read *Italian Princess*. Again, everyone thought we were sisters, and we did nothing to dissuade them. When we were out anywhere, people would first ask if we were sisters and then ask me where I was from. I'd say my family was from Bari, which was a city in southern Italy. This was my excuse to become someone else, and being an Italian princess suited me just fine.

On some days, particularly the hot ones, Lisa and I would go to her house after school to hang out at her pool. One especially hot afternoon, we picked up some Bartles & Jaymes wine coolers, which were popular at the time, and sipped them through straws while floating on rafts. We thought sipping our drinks through straws would prevent us from getting drunk. We thought wrong. The next thing I knew, it was time for my dad to pick me up, so I ran into Lisa's room, changed out of my bikini, put my uniform back on, and sobered up quickly. I was, essentially, living a double life. I was one person at school and someone else at home. In some ways, I had become my father.

My mother decided to throw me a sweet sixteen birthday party, which, instead of looking forward to, I absolutely dreaded. After all, my birthday parties were more for my mother than for me. She'd invite all her friends from the

Muslim community and their daughters, whom I had nothing in common with.

"Why are you even doing this?" I asked angrily.

"They're girls your age," she replied. "You should be friends with them." She was unrelenting in her belief that she could make me be friends with them, but the more she tried, the more I resisted. One of her tactics was telling me that I would never be accepted by the girls at school.

"Don't try to be like them," she'd say. "You can't keep up. You will never be one of them." She would go back to this negative mantra over and over again in an effort to discourage me.

When I wasn't at Lisa's house, I'd hide out in my room, which was still decorated in the pink, red, and green from my childhood. I hated it. Finally, I persuaded my mother to let me update it, and when I say "let me," I mean let her and her friend Emma take the lead. Thankfully, they allowed me to choose a proper bed with a headboard and side tables, and I was even more relieved when they ripped out the ugly red carpet. They painted the walls a light teal with a matching carpet and bought all-white lacquer furniture, befitting a bedroom designed by a woman with even bigger hair than mine.

During high school, my mother's criticism of me went from harsh comments to outright yelling. The house, normally as quiet as a morgue, would erupt into screaming matches between us. I wanted her to accept me for who I was; she refused. She'd list all the ways "we" were better than Westerners. We didn't eat pork and we didn't do this or that, and on and on it would go. I felt completely unseen, like who I was and what I liked didn't matter in the least.

"But that isn't who I am!" I'd yell.

"You're following the devil's path!" she'd threaten. Often, her complaints were focused on my friendship with Lisa, and how it was negatively shaping who I was becoming.

"You're never going to be free like her," she'd say.

"If you hate it so much here, why'd you even come to the U.S.?" I'd ask. "Why not just move back to India?!"

Sometimes, she'd go into my father's study and complain about me to him. Quietly, he'd listen to her go on and on until finally he'd snap.

"That's enough!" I'd hear him say.

It's not even that he didn't agree with her. He just didn't agree with her rigidity or harsh comments. He also would have liked me to be friends with the other Muslim girls. He also would have liked me to embrace Islam, but he was more accepting of who I was than she. He was proud of me, even if I wasn't exactly the way he wanted me to be.

The tension between my mother and me probably wasn't helped by the fact that my father and I had a special relationship that grew stronger as I got older. When he needed help, he would come to me instead of to her, because I knew how to do things. Often, I would go shopping with him and help him pick out clothes. If we needed a new VCR for the TV or some other electronic device, I'd research it and install it. His desk was a mess, so I helped him organize it, getting him bookshelves and creating a filing system.

Later, I'd accompany him on his business trips and help him with social interactions and professional introductions. He relied on me for these things, and I enjoyed doing them, but, over time, a dynamic was created within our family that I would be the go-to person to handle everything. I would be the one who could help. This worked until it didn't—until, many years later, the burden and responsibility would become so overwhelming, it almost broke me—but, for now, it felt good. It brought us closer together. That doesn't mean our relationship was without conflict. Especially when, at age 17, I went against his wishes and finally got that job I wanted.

It was only a part-time summer job at a local jewelry shop, but he was not happy when he found out. I wasn't supposed to work because I was a doctor's daughter, after all. Volunteering at the hospital was respectable; working retail was not. In their eyes, everything I did reflected on them, but I knew I couldn't let this stop me. I was a good student. I never got in trouble. The more I got away from them and exposed myself to new experiences, the more I would learn and grow.

However, what I learned from working in retail was that I wasn't cut out for customer service. I wanted to be of service, but piercing someone's ears is a far cry from being in the operating room during surgery. I had a yearning to be a part of something bigger—bigger than working a job with no meaningful connection and bigger than living my whole life on the same island I grew up on.

The following year, I joined the junior prom planning committee. I may not be cut out for retail, but I am cut out for getting things done and doing so in a way that hasn't been done before—a fact that contributed to my career success for years to come—even though I didn't know it at the time. What I did know was that accepting the status quo was not something I was interested in.

"We're getting off of Staten Island," I announced to the prom committee.

In past years, prom was always held on Staten Island. Not this year. I booked the ballroom at the iconic Pierre Hotel in Manhattan, known for being the home to celebrities like Coco Chanel, Elizabeth Taylor, and Barbra Streisand. Even though Manhattan was only eighteen miles from Staten Island, it was worlds away in terms of sophistication and culture, and I couldn't wait to live in a place like that. Prom may have been a small step into that world, but I couldn't wait to get away from the small-minded bullying of our across-the-street neighbors, the unrelenting harassment of my mother, and the subservient and oppressive culture that became my experience of Islam. But first I needed to learn how to drive.

CHAPTER EIGHT

FOR SOME REASON, WHEN it was time for me to learn how to drive, my mother also decided she wanted to learn how to drive. I guess she was finally tired of either relying on my dad or taking taxis everywhere. Even though my mother was religiously conservative and didn't agree with Western cultural norms, she had her convenient exceptions, such as wearing pants, getting manicures, and cutting her hair short, along with regular visits to the salon. By the 1980s, she decided to add driving to that very limited list.

While I was taking my driver's ed class at St. Clotilde's, she enrolled in a private driving school. When she was ready—or rather, when she thought she was—she decided to pick me up from high school in her brand-new Cutlass Ciera. I was not thrilled by this idea.

As my classmates waited for their rides or hung out on the front lawn of the school, I waited for my mother with trepidation. Finally, I saw my mother's Cutlass slowly come down the street and approach the campus with its left signal blinking. She had brought her friend for moral support—this was the same friend who had hosted the dinner party where I was assaulted.

I watched my mother slowly pull into the turn lane and wait for the oncoming traffic to clear. After many missed opportunities, she accelerated slowly, while her friend chattered away next to her. I held my breath as I watched her grip the steering wheel to make the turn. The car approached the driveway, went up the curb, and crashed into a brick wall in slow motion. I wanted to disappear.

Another time, she and this same friend decided to drive into New York City to shop at the luxury department store Bloomingdale's, located on the East Side of Manhattan. They got on the Staten Island Expressway and took the exit for Bloomingdale Road, thinking that, obviously, Bloomingdale's would be located on Bloomingdale Road. It's not. In fact, it's in the exact opposite direction. They ended up in an undeveloped area on another part of the island and were lost for hours. It was times like these that I wondered how we could possibly be mother and daughter. We were different in every way possible.

Perhaps this is why she tried to stop me from being friends with Lisa. Lisa and I had a closeness that she and I would never have. Even Lisa's parents and I had trust and affection, and that was impossible with her. Lisa and I felt like family in a way my mother and I would never be. This came to a head after an incident at school that ended up in the local newspaper.

Some boys from St. Vitus High School got into an argument and, as is the case with high school, the boys had planned to meet behind St. Clotilde's Academy to fight it out. Word spread, and hundreds of kids from various schools gathered on Victory Boulevard to witness the big fight. I was there, of course, with Lisa and a few girls from our school. Anticipation and excitement grew. The nuns came running. The principal and residents called the police. Soon sirens were blaring and everyone scattered. Later, my parents heard about it. Several kids from various schools got into trouble and I was "forbidden" from hanging out with Lisa.

"But it's not her fault! She had nothing to do with it," I said.

"She's a bad influence," retorted my mother. "She's like the ringleader. She tells you what to do and you do it."

Nothing I said would change my parents' minds, and nothing they said would make me stop hanging out with Lisa.

"So they think I'm a bad seed?" Lisa asked me.

"Yep," I said.

Ultimately, Lisa and I would just laugh about it. What else could you do? My parents didn't know then that Lisa would be there for me throughout the rest of our lives, and she'd be there for them, too, until the very end. These conflicts, if anything, drove me away from home even more. Soon, my mother and I were fighting about my curfew, which was much earlier than my friends'. It wasn't like I stayed out super late; I would just typically come home a half hour after curfew.

"I've been waiting for you," yelled my mother.

"Who asked you to?" I'd respond angrily. Finally, I bargained with them. "Let's think about this for a moment," I'd say calmly. "Clearly, coming home a half hour after curfew is a trend. Perhaps you should think of what time you want me to come home and then just add thirty minutes to it because that's when I'll realistically be coming home." It seemed like a reasonable solution to me.

Another negotiation was what college I would go to. Of course, I wanted to go as far away as possible, and, of course, my parents wanted me as close to them as possible. I even ordered a catalog from the University of Hawaii thinking that seemed a good distance from them, but, honestly, I knew it was between Boston University, Penn State, and NYU. My dad suggested Hofstra College on Long Island, which was about thirty miles away so I could come home on the weekends and even offered to buy me a new car to sweeten the deal. I agreed to visit the school, which turned out to be (at least in my eyes at the time) the Long Island version of Staten Island. It was a nonstarter.

After checking out Penn State, I got ready for my trip to Boston University, where I had heard the students were much more conservative and preppy. I purchased a buttoned-up polyester blouse from a local store and wore it with a long, pleated skirt and heels so that I would fit in. Though the skirt was thick and heavy, my mother insisted I wear a long slip under it. It wasn't worth another fight, so I did.

When we got to the airport, I started running so I could make it to the gate on time. Suddenly, my slip fell. I tried pulling it up as I ran, but it gathered around my knees until it fell to my ankles, causing me to career to the floor, flat on my face in the middle of the terminal in front of seemingly hundreds of travelers. The slip literally made me slip. I ripped it off, threw it in the trash, and kept running. I have never worn one since.

When I arrived in Boston, I became enveloped in a sea of whiteness. It wasn't snow; it was a lack of diversity. I had experienced enough of that in Staten Island. I would have to look elsewhere.

New York University checked all my boxes except for the fact that it was only a short ferry ride from my parents' home—which was much too close. But the student body was diverse and the campus expansive—far larger than anything I had experienced previously. NYU is centered in the thriving historic and cultural neighborhoods of Greenwich Village and Washington Square Park in New York City, and the faculty boasts notable scholars and professionals working at the top of their fields. My parents were thrilled. Thus began the negotiations.

"I'll go to NYU with one provision," I said. "I'm not going to live at home and commute. Instead, I'm going to live in the dorms."

"But you'll come home on the weekends," they countered.

"I'll come home on *some* weekends," I replied.

Finally, we came to an agreement.

I couldn't wait to experience everything the university and city had to offer. I couldn't wait to finally be free—even if not completely. That freedom would take longer, and it wouldn't be easy. There would be a price to pay.

Before a caterpillar turns into a butterfly, it dissolves into nothingness. That's what my senior year in high school felt like. Would I indeed turn into a butterfly? Would I experience a metamorphosis? My anger and resistance toward my mother had fueled me throughout school. Her betrayal, her never-ending criticisms, her insistence that I was wrong if I didn't adopt her religion and culture (which, to me, were one and the same), and her denial of the person that I truly am drove me to excel until I finally hit a wall and completely shut down. The catalyst was an incident with a girl who spread lies about me behind my back.

One afternoon at school, everyone was hanging out in the school lounge and the phone rang. Someone answered it and said it was for me. She said it was a boy. I was confused. No one called me there—much less a boy. When I answered the phone, the boy asked me to go out.

"I don't know you," I said.

"Well, I know all about you," he replied, creepily. I quickly hung up.

Then the phone rang again. Another girl answered it and, again, she said it was for me. It was another boy. I refused to answer. She hung up and the phone rang again and again and again. All these boys were calling and asking for me. It was embarrassing, and I was shattered. I knew something had happened—that something was being said about me. But what, and, most of all, why? I didn't do anything to give anyone a reason to talk badly about me. I wasn't promiscuous. I was a good girl.

"Don't let it bother you," my friends said, consolingly, but how could I not? School had been my one safe place, the place that I would escape to, and now even that was violated. Lisa was upset too. She knew it was ridiculous. The boys were from St. Vitus, so she told our friend, Ethan, who quickly found out what happened.

One of the girls who was part of our larger friend group had spread a rumor at St. Vitus saying that I was "easy." I don't know why she wanted to humiliate me, but she had, and I was furious. I was hurt, and I was done. It was then that I began to withdraw into myself.

One evening, Ethan pulled up in front of my house in his white pickup truck, and I came out to talk to him like we always did, but, this time, it was under different circumstances. He saw that I was upset and told me that he had talked to the other boys and straightened them out. Ethan was and still is a friend.

From that day on, I never said another word to that girl. I didn't look at her or acknowledge her existence in any way. I was done with her. I don't know if this is a shortcoming or not, but if someone betrays my trust, I close the door, forever and without an ounce of remorse.

That incident triggered an avalanche of memories containing everything that had happened to me growing up, and I retreated into myself. I stopped hanging out in the lounge and, instead, would find an empty classroom to go into and read. I stopped going out with Lisa or anyone else. After school, I'd go home and stay in my room. I was done. Everything inside me was screaming "Get me out of here!" I knew I had to leave. I knew I had to go someplace bigger—someplace where I could be my own person.

At this point, I had received my acceptance letter to NYU, but that also filled me with anxiety and trepidation. What would that be like? Who would I become? I fell into a low-grade depression, and everything seemed to turn in on me. The fire that raged inside of me, that had kept me going, seemed to have died. Nothing was left to fuel me. I was in the cocoon—no longer a caterpillar and not yet a butterfly. I felt alone in the dark, dissolving into nothingness.

A couple of people helped during this time. Lisa, of course, knew something was wrong but also knew me well enough to give me the space that I needed. Occasionally, she'd check up on me and let me know that she loved me.

"I'm here for you whenever you need me," she'd say, "but I don't want to be a pain in the ass and get you mad at me!" She gave me space.

Then, one day, one of my favorite English teachers noticed that something was wrong. I had taken all his classes, so he knew me well. After class, he asked me to stay and talk, and, through our conversations, I was finally able to open up to him as a much-needed objective outsider about what had been going on at home. I was finally able to talk about my anxiety and stress about the future. Up to then, I hadn't told anyone about any of it. I kept everything separate. There was school and there was home. I didn't tell anyone, not even Lisa, about the neighborhood bullying, what happened to me in Saudi Arabia, or my mother's constant harassment. When it came down to it, I was embarrassed and ashamed. It was easier to just keep it all inside—until it wasn't.

During this time, I kept my focus on graduation and got through the rest of the semester on autopilot. My mantras were "I'm done," and "Get me out of here."

As we were in rehearsal for our graduation ceremony, all the girls were talking about the dresses they were going to wear, getting their hair and nails done, or the color of their corsages. I didn't want any of that. I wanted to do it my own way. Most of the girls in my larger friend group were going to stay on Staten Island to go to college, and I just couldn't relate.

On the day of graduation, instead of wearing a dress and corsage, I walked across the stage wearing a white skirt suit and holding a single rose instead of a corsage. After the ceremony, while everyone hung out with their families, taking pictures, and chatting, I just wanted to leave. My father politely said hello to parents and teachers, and my mother was her usual unapproachable self even though she had known everyone since I was in kindergarten. My goal was to get out of there as quickly as possible. I said a quick goodbye to Mary and Lisa and then, with my parents following, I walked out the door and didn't look back.

My withdrawal into myself wasn't submission. I would never submit to my mother or to a religion or anything else. Instead, my withdrawal was a way to survive until I could regroup and find a way out. It was a strategy that served me well then and into the future.

I didn't know what college life would bring. What would it be like to live in a cramped dorm room with two girls I didn't even know? What would it be like living in the heart of the city, going to school with the best students from all over the world? All I knew was that I was ready to put everything bad behind me. I was ready to make my own life. My chrysalis was breaking, and I was ready to fly.

PART TWO

My First Tastes
of Freedom

CHAPTER NINE

"HOW DO YOU KNOW him?" my parents asked in a concerned tone. They were referring to Charles, who saw me hauling my belongings up the stairs into my new college dorm and offered to help. Charles was just a friend of my cousin's from high school whom I occasionally ran into, but this was their response to any boy that I happened to know. Boys and girls were not supposed to be friends. I was glad he offered to help since my parents weren't the physical type, and it would be left to me to carry everything into the small room that would be my new home for the next year.

All I knew was that I wanted as much independence as I could get and, to prove my newfound independence, I only took what I needed from their house—my clothes and necessary personal items. I left everything else behind. My dad may have been paying for my tuition and housing, but I insisted on paying for everything else. I thought this would make me less beholden to them. This didn't stop their ongoing demands, and the outrageousness of their demands wouldn't come to a head until I graduated. But, in the meantime, I was finally out of my parents' house. I was free . . . or free-*ish*.

The question: "How do you know him?" was a common one with my parents. Any time I mentioned a guy, or talked to one, it was a huge deal. It was as if I should only know girls and avoid all boys. Charles was just a handsome and polite young man helping their daughter and, instead of being appreciative, they were suspicious.

"How do you know him?!" my mother asked again. I sighed. I had already answered a barrage of questions during our drive from Staten Island to Greenwich Village. It just wouldn't stop.

"Is the dorm co-ed? Are the boys on a separate floor?"

My parents were in for a rude awakening.

"You mean there are boys on the same floor as you?!" they gasped, staring at the co-ed undergrads streaming into Rubin Hall followed by parents seemingly unconcerned by mixed-gender cohabitation. Little did they know that I would soon become better friends with the guys living on the third floor than the girls in my own room.

You would think that I would be nervous going from a graduating class of ninety-two girls to a university with over twenty-eight thousand undergrads, but I was ready for it. I was ready to be with some of the top students from around the world. I was ready to be inspired by professors who were at the top of their fields and careers. I was ready to explore this city full of eight million people from every imaginable background. What I wasn't ready for was Layla.

Living in a small dorm room with two other girls is very different from living in your own bedroom. There were two twin beds, two desks, and a twin bed-desk loft—but we did have a view of Fifth Avenue. The first roommate I met was Elizabeth. She was Danish by heritage but grew up in Sparta, New Jersey, and was as sweet as sweet can be. Even though we ended up not hanging out much, she was easy to live with.

Layla was another story. Everything about her was sharp—her features, her personality, and her attitude. It was clear from the start that we were not going to like each other, let alone be friends. On top of that, she always had her boyfriend, Chet, over. Chet didn't get along with his roommates and so decided to take up residence with Layla in our room. One of the ways I dealt with that was by being there as little as possible.

Fortunately, I quickly met Dave and Johnny, who both lived on the third floor. Johnny was from Connecticut and Dave was from Long Island, and they had just become roommates and fast friends. It wasn't long before we were inseparable. It was one of those friendships that just clicked, and even though our friendship was purely platonic, "how do you know those boys?!" became my mother's constant refrain over the scores of times she met them.

She had no frame of reference for male friendship. In fact, it was essentially forbidden in her upbringing and culture, yet it always came naturally to me. The three of us would hang out all day and night. We'd hang out on weekends doing everything or nothing at all. We'd talk about everything or nothing, and, most of all, we'd laugh.

So, even though I was virtually never in my dorm room, I still had to sleep there, and having Chet there all the time got old quickly. If Layla and he weren't cooking in the room, leaving our bedding and clothes stinky, they were having sex while I was trying to sleep. I am a calm person normally, but this was too much. They were violating my living space and privacy. I lost it.

"Chet can't be here all the time!" I yelled at Layla. "This is my room, too, and I want him out!" Layla didn't care. She just yelled back until it became a screaming match and Johnny and Dave came and grabbed me out of there. If I looked to Elizabeth for support, she would kind of agree but ultimately remain neutral. She just didn't want to get involved. I was at a loss.

The breaking point came when my father saw my phone bill from the landline he had put in the room. One day, I saw that Layla had been using my phone to make long-lasting, long-distance calls costing hundreds of dollars while I was in class or somewhere else. When my dad saw the bill and I told him she made the calls, he became angry. When I added that she was having sex with her boyfriend in the bed right next to me, it put him over the edge—as I knew it would. The university moved her out of the dorm not long after.

Even though I was finally living away from home, I was still only a short ferry ride from my parents. They would either come to visit me or expect me to come home every other weekend. One weekend, while they were visiting, I introduced them to a Pakistani boy who was also living in the co-ed dorm. They had already met Johnny and Dave, and I wanted to prove to them that even Muslim boys lived here. They immediately liked him even though they knew nothing about him.

"Do you hang out with him a lot?" they asked, excitedly.

The truth was we didn't hang out at all, and I don't even recall his name. He wasn't a "hang out" kind of guy and, when it came down to it, we didn't have that much in common. I had more in common with Johnny and Dave than I did with him. My parents were out of luck.

~

The coping mechanisms that I had developed during high school came in handy in college. Basically, what my parents didn't know wouldn't hurt them. I may have gone to parties and clubs when I was a teenager, but it wasn't because I was rebelling against my parents. It was because I wanted to, and it was fun—and I still got good grades. The same was true while I was attending NYU, and my first year was a whirlwind.

On top of taking a full course load, I couldn't wait to check out the city nightlife. I went to nightclubs like the Limelight, which used to be an Episcopal Church originally built in 1844, and Studio 54, which was made famous by the likes of Diana Ross, Jacqueline Kennedy Onassis, Cher, and Andy Warhol. Every night I went out, I was surrounded by dancing bodies writhing and sweating on the world's most famous dance floors and hanging out in lounges catering to every type of scene and clique.

It's not unusual for first-year college students to burn the candle at both ends, and I was no exception. As long as my grades were good and I was having fun, I didn't care—until I woke up so exhausted and sick I could barely get out of bed. It turns out I had mononucleosis—widely referred to as the kissing disease because it's spread through saliva. It can just as easily be caught by sharing food or utensils with someone, but my father was still furious.

"How do you have the kissing disease?!" he demanded.

"I'm just tired," I replied.

The truth was I had run myself ragged. I started spending more time at the library and less time at the clubs.

Then I met my first real boyfriend.

Dating Kevin was probably part of my rebellion. We met in Washington Square Park which is in the heart of NYU's sprawling New York City campus. He wasn't a college student; he wasn't my age, and he certainly wasn't Muslim. Instead, he was a 23-year-old New York City police officer from, of all places, Staten Island. He was also very handsome. In some ways, he had a dangerous edge to him that made him attractive in a bad-boy kind of way, and it wouldn't be an exaggeration to say that he was not the best police officer on the force. In fact, his tenure with the department was short-lived. Yet when I was with him, I felt safe and protected. I had no problem introducing him to Dave, Johnny, Lisa, or anyone else, for that matter—anyone except my parents, of course.

To say that my parents would have been unhappy that my boyfriend was a white New York City police officer is a major understatement. They would have been horrified. He conveniently checked all the boxes of what my parents didn't want for me and, in retrospect, dating him was a way to stake out my independence and forcibly reject all that my parents wanted. Welcome to adulthood.

My life was turning into what I had always dreamed of. It was engaging and exciting, and, most of all, I was free of the small-mindedness of my mother and the neighborhood bullies. Not only was I studying with the best and the brightest, I was also frequently among celebrities—whether it was on the dance floor, at a cool new restaurant, or even on campus.

One night when Kevin and I were having a late-night bite at a local restaurant in Washington Square, one of the founding members of the hit rock band Huey Lewis and the News walked in and we joined him for a drink. It was commonplace to see the late John F. Kennedy Jr. studying at the NYU Law Library or the actress Kristen Johnston in Rubin Hall. She would go on to win two Emmys for her role in the popular TV show *3rd Rock from the Sun*, and would frequently step over our legs as Johnny, Dave, and I sat on the floor of the dorm hallway talking. I was definitely not in Staten Island anymore.

CHAPTER TEN

I WAS EXPERIENCING A lot of exciting firsts, but I was taken by surprise when my first breakup happened. One evening, Kevin sat me down and told me he had decided to get back together with his ex-girlfriend and that it probably wasn't a good idea for me to be dating someone like him. I was devastated but, deep down, I knew he was right. I buried myself in my studies even more, and, in no time, bounced back. With my first heartache out of the way, I set my sights on gaining even more independence.

I always knew financial freedom was the key to independence. The more money I had, the more options I would have. As I started my second year at NYU, I decided to take the graveyard shift in the emergency room at the Staten Island hospital where I had previously volunteered. Every Thursday to Sunday night for the next year and a half, I'd take the Staten Island Ferry home and go straight to the hospital for my shift that started at 11 p.m. and ended at 7 a.m. the next morning. Then I'd go home to sleep and study and do it again until Monday morning, when my mother would drive me to the Staten Island Ferry so I could make it to my Monday afternoon classes. My goal to make and save money fueled me.

Another step toward independence was moving into a different dorm and having only one roommate instead of two. My new roommate, Amelia, was a busty platinum blonde who came from a family involved in politics. That January, we headed to her hometown of D.C., where we volunteered for George Bush's inauguration, and I soon found myself in the White House stuffing gift bags. Amelia was a lot of fun and a great roommate, but I found myself wanting my own space. I was just not cut out for roommates. I set my sights on getting the rare and highly prized single dorm room.

In the meantime, I focused on experiencing everything that college life had to offer. One afternoon, I was walking across the park and came upon a rush event where all the school's sororities and fraternities tried to recruit new pledges. Realizing I had not made any girlfriends in college because of the incident with Ana in high school, I decided to look around. Instead of the "mean girls" that I expected, I found a group of girls who were down-to-earth and engaging. I imagined that these girls could become lifelong friends, and even though I loved hanging out with Johnny and Dave, I hadn't had a lot of girlfriends other than my close friendship with Lisa. I decided to pledge Alpha Phi Zeta.

As with many things, I told my parents after I was initiated. It wasn't worth all the questions and arguments. They would say that I was being frivolous and that joining a sorority would distract me from my studies. They were already mad that I wasn't coming home as frequently as they wanted, and they knew I was being exposed to things outside of their control and comfort zone. I wasn't about to rub salt into their wounds by telling them something that I was going to do anyway. It was better to go ahead and pledge and then tell them later when I got in.

During my second year, I started taking my classes more seriously, even though my grades were already good, and I was a year ahead of my class thanks to my AP and college bridge classes from high school. Since most of my classes during the first year were larger survey courses, I felt excited by the idea of diving deeper into my field of study in my second year. As a journalism major, I was taking a magazine writing class and was looking for something interesting to write about. The Body Shop had just opened its flagship store in NYC with a not-so-common mission at the time. They were going to sell products that were ethically sourced, cruelty-free, and contained only natural ingredients. I wanted to learn more.

I decided that the best way to proceed would be to interview the British owner, the late Anita Roddick, so I called their corporate headquarters and introduced myself. Much to my surprise, her office returned my call. My roommate, Amelia, picked up the phone and pretended to be my secretary. We set up a meeting and I met Roddick in person at her new Manhattan store. After the interview and writing up the article, I realized that this was what I wanted to do. I didn't just want to report the facts, I wanted to interact with people and bring things to life. Little did I know that this experience would foreshadow more to come.

Being able to brush shoulders with movers and shakers in the world of business and journalism thrilled me, and NYU offered me just that. One of my classes was taught by Jon Katz, who wrote and produced for renowned outlets like The Washington Post, The Boston Globe, and CBS News. We'd sit in class banging on our typewriters, hammering out articles, and learning the tricks of the trade. For example, if we were writing a story about an apartment building fire, we were told that we needed to ask the tenants how they felt about it, because that was part of the story.

"How do they feel?" I asked, aghast.

This seemed like exactly what you would *not* want to do. It felt intrusive and insensitive. That realization was pivotal for me. It was like the time I volunteered in the hospital's memory care center and brought food to the woman who couldn't remember me from one day to the next. I wasn't cut out for that, and I wasn't cut out for this. I cared too much. I wanted to help people, but not like this. So how could I make a difference? It was a question I would struggle with until I finally got my first break.

∼

Being in a sorority didn't change my experience of college as much as I thought it would. Because I was a year older than most of the pledges, I felt drawn to the founding sisters who were older and getting ready to graduate. Another reason was that by the time they opened the new sorority house a few blocks away from campus, I had finally scored my own private dorm room in Stern Hall located right across from Washington Square Park and next to the library. My windows looked out onto the trees outside, and I finally had the privacy I craved.

As graduation was approaching, I didn't feel ready to start my post-college life. There were still so many classes I wanted to take and so much I wanted to experience. Even though I was busy, I decided to join the student council because I knew it would give me leadership experience and look good on a resume. Again, I found myself overextended and exhausted, but I was hungry for everything college life had to offer.

I started to panic. What was I going to do? Where would I work? I decided to stay an extra semester and graduate after the following fall term. This would leave me the summer and fall to figure things out. My parents assumed I'd come home for the summer, but what would I do there? There was no way I was going back there.

Instead, I applied to be a resident assistant for my dorm so I could stay there for free during the summer. This allowed me to keep my independence and take away any cause for my dad to complain, since he wasn't paying for my dorm. He and my mother were not thrilled by this. Since I didn't have a lot of money, I lived on a dollar a day. That afforded me a "dirty water" dog, which was a boiled hot dog from a street vendor that had sat soaking in water all day. I wouldn't eat them today, but back then, it was worth the price of my freedom.

During the summer, I was the only one left in the dorm building, but I was not alone. My sorority was friendly with certain fraternities, and one of them was FIJI, whose house was only a block from my dorm and much closer than the sorority house. I became friends with many of the FIJI brothers, so, during the summer, it was where I went to hang out. It was comfortable and full of camaraderie.

In the afternoons, I would work at the front desk of Stern Hall and, since there was nothing really to do, I would bury my nose in a textbook. It would have been pretty lonely if it wasn't for Scot, one of my friends from FIJI, who would come by and study with me. Hours would pass as we'd sit quietly studying, and it made the time pass quickly. Sometimes, though, I just needed a break.

One balmy summer evening, I closed my book. I was tired of studying. I was tired of dirty water dogs. I was tired of thinking about the future. I went over to FIJI, and it looked like I wasn't the only one who felt that way. We all needed a break. Since it was nice out, I suggested that we walk to the Empire State Building before it closed and go to the rooftop lookout.

A large group of us quickly formed, and together we walked the ten-plus blocks to West 34th Street and rode the elevator to the top floor. Looking out over the city lights, I felt hopeful for the future. A momentary peace washed over me, replacing the anxiety and stress that I usually felt. The normally raucous group of friends became quiet as we took in the beauty of the city below us—the city that had become our home, at least for now.

We took that walk many more times that year. It was as if being on top of the Empire State Building gave our lives perspective. That everything would be okay. That there was nothing to worry about. We had an unobstructed view all the way uptown and all the way down to the World Trade Center's Twin Towers. We didn't know what the future would bring, but, in those moments, it seemed bright.

The camaraderie that I found with the guys in FIJI was an unexpected plus of joining the sorority. The reason it was so easy and fun was probably because it was purely platonic.

I am still friends with some of the guys, going to their weddings, and exchanging holiday cards and pictures of our kids. I may not have found my lifelong tribe of close female friends at the sorority, but that would come later.

CHAPTER ELEVEN

THE YEAR BEFORE I graduated, the movie *Working Girl* was nominated for six Academy Awards. It depicts a young blue-collar woman from Staten Island trying to work her way up the corporate ladder in Manhattan. It starred Melanie Griffith and featured big hair, the female power suit, and the evil female boss. Apparently, it was inspired by the trend of female commuters wearing sneakers with their skirt suits and carrying their high heels in their bags.

I didn't relate to Melanie Griffith's character with her Staten Island accent, which brought nothing but bad associations. What I would relate to, unfortunately, was having an abusive female boss.

My first internship was at a renowned PR agency on Park Avenue South—home of the power suit. I purchased my office attire from the low-end clothing shops on Sixth Avenue, which was all I could afford at the time. All I knew was that I wanted to be seen as an adult and taken seriously. My assignment for the six-week unpaid internship was to create a clipbook for an automotive clear coat company that contained all their print media coverage. It was the least interesting thing I could imagine doing, but I discovered something that I did like, though: working in a dynamic professional environment.

Park Avenue South is blocks from NYU, but it couldn't be more different. Tall buildings tower above crowded sidewalks filled with business people rushing from the subway to their offices. It was intimidating yet thrilling. I knew I wanted to be part of that someday—and not just any part—I wanted to be the boss.

However, in 1989, there was no #girlboss, and no internet. Cell phones and computers were considered a new technology. Though I was inspired by the people and professors around me, I didn't see them as role models. In fact, I didn't really see anyone who looked like me making it big in business or journalism, but instead of allowing my energy to be drained by that reality, I put everything I had into becoming the strong, independent person of my dreams.

One of the first places where I got a taste of that power was on my father's business trips, where I would be his "plus one." I started going with him during my second year at NYU, and the first one I attended was at the luxurious Ritz-Carlton in Naples, Florida. The food was amazing, the cocktail hour was elegant, and the conversations were engaging. This was a far cry from the Islamic Medical Association conferences that I'd been dragged to when I was a kid. Instead of having to be quiet, not make eye contact, and cover my arms, legs, and head, I was able to actively engage in conversations with other physicians, dress how I wanted, and laugh as loud as I pleased. And, since my dad wasn't as talkative or outgoing as I was, I would play the social hostess and make introductions.

It was something I was good at, and it was fun. It also felt good to be appreciated by my father.

These experiences informed my thinking as post-college life rapidly approached. I had found some things I liked, such as being social, helping people, and working in a dynamic professional environment. And, since I had taken so many classes, I ended up with two minors—political science and speech communications—on top of my journalism major. In mulling over jobs, I crossed newscaster off my list because I would have to move to a small market in the middle of nowhere and make around $13,000 a year, which, even though it was quite a while ago, was still not a lot of money. Plus, the odds of a woman of color being hired to do the news—or even accepted—in small-town USA in the late '80s and early '90s were not exactly high, nor was the salary or living situation desirable to me, especially after living in New York City.

My next step was to grab the New York Times classifieds and look for a job in publishing. What I found were a bunch of entry-level jobs that required high words-per-minute typing skills. I couldn't type that fast, and I wasn't thrilled at the prospect of learning how to. My father suggested that I could get a job at his hospital, but I wanted to work in my field of study. I wanted to carve out my own path, and I certainly didn't want to end up back in Staten Island living at home with my mother's constant criticisms, the racism and bullying from my neighbors, and the overall feeling of suffocation. I had gotten a taste of living on my own in one of the most exciting cities in the world and rubbing shoulders with world-renowned scholars and professionals. How could I go back to Staten Island?

Graduation day quickly came, and I joined the rest of the graduates who took over Washington Square Park for the ceremonies. As I looked across the sea of purple robes and out into the large audience made up of friends and families, I felt proud of what I had accomplished, but that pride was tempered by sadness that it was over and anxiety about what was to come. As the ceremony came to a close, I joined the rest of the graduates mingling through the crowd in search of their parents and marveled at how different this felt from my high school graduation. Instead of wanting to flee, I wanted to revel in the last moments of college life. My cozy little dorm room overlooking the park, my friends Dave and Johnny, my sisters at Alpha Phi Zeta, my friends at FIJI, the city that overflowed with promise and possibility—it was time to leave all that behind and, yes, move back home with my parents.

CHAPTER TWELVE

"WE WANT TO TALK to you about something," my mother said two weeks after I moved home with them after graduation.

"Uh-oh," I thought.

We had just finished dinner, and I was watching TV with my dad in his study. My mother came in and sat in her chair next to me. Then my father got up from his desk and sat next to me on the couch, which was when I knew that whatever was about to happen was serious.

My mother continued: "Now that you're done with school, we need to talk about you getting married," she said.

"What?!" I sputtered, incredulously.

"It's time for you to get married," my mother repeated.

"What are you talking about?" I exclaimed. "I have a career ahead of me. How can you even suggest that?" My normally calm and controlled demeanor quickly turned into outrage.

"It's time," she insisted.

To be clear, they weren't talking about me finding a really

great guy, dating, and then getting married. They were talking about an arranged marriage.

"We've never had this conversation before," I said. "Why did I even go to college?!" My outrage turned into sobs.

She was unrelenting. I looked at my father through my tears. He was the one you could reason with. If my mother was a dictator, he was the diplomat.

"We're not saying that you have to marry this person; we're just saying that we want you to meet him," my father said calmly.

"Meet *him*?!" I was flabbergasted. They had already found someone. This had all been planned.

I glared at them. "If you wanted this kind of life for me, why did you even come to the U.S.? Why did you dangle this life in front of me if you were just going to take it away?"

They wouldn't budge. It was time to negotiate. It felt like my whole relationship with my parents was a negotiation. It's probably where I first learned how to do it.

"Fine," I relented. "Talk me through the process."

I was told that to find a suitable mate, parents typically reach out to their network. During that process, my mother had found a woman whom she had gone to elementary school with. And that woman had a son in Tennessee who wanted to get married. Yay me.

My mother handed me a black-and-white photo of a stern-looking man in a three-piece suit who had a receding hairline. If it were today, I would have swiped left without batting an eye. Handwritten on the back of the photo were the names of his mother and father, his paternal and maternal grandparents, his education, and the education and profes-sions of his father and grandfathers. In arranged marriages, only people of similar backgrounds are supposed to marry in order to maintain the same social status or attain a better one. It didn't matter that the picture of this stranger felt repulsive to me or that the idea of marrying him felt emotionally and intellectually repugnant. The last thing that I wanted was to end up like my mother, miserable and sheltered. I had a life to live. However, my parents had already arranged for us to meet the following month.

I started to lay out my terms.

"I'm not going to dress in traditional clothing or change my personality," I said.

"Fine," they said.

"I don't want to be left alone with him," I added.

"We need you to spend some time alone with him so you can get to know him," they countered.

"But not for very long, and you won't be far, right?" I asked.

"We'll be just down the hall," they answered.

"I also don't want to sit near him during any meals," I said.

They paused.

"If you want this, these are my terms," I added. They acquiesced.

February came quicker than I would have liked. Much to my relief, my father booked the guy and his mother a hotel room so they wouldn't have to stay with us. But luck was not on my side: a huge snowstorm was forecasted to hit shortly after their arrival.

"What if they get stuck at their hotel?" worried my mother.

"Too bad!" I exclaimed. "They can't stay here with us." I looked at my father.

"If it snows, I won't be able to get them from the hotel," he replied. "They have to stay here."

It felt like my world was collapsing in on me.

"I do not want to do this," I said. "I'll be pleasant, for your sake, but that is it."

I didn't tell anyone about this—not even Lisa. It felt humiliating. When I did eventually tell her, her mouth dropped. She was aghast. We were the same age, living in the same country, but it was like we were living in two different worlds.

The day of their arrival came, and my mother found herself face-to-face with a woman even more traditional than she was. This former childhood classmate looked at my mother's short haircut, makeup, and jewelry with an unmasked sneer. In her eyes, my mother's appearance was improper. We all went into the living room and sat down. The woman was wearing a traditional sari with sandals and socks, even though there was snow outside. She wore no makeup, and her hair was pulled back tightly into a bun. Her son wore the same three-piece suit that was in the picture I had first seen.

The conversation proceeded awkwardly as I put a fake smile on my face and counted the minutes. The son turned to me. "I understand you just graduated from college. What was your major?" he asked.

"Journalism," I responded, politely.

"Why would you study something as frivolous as that?" he said with a sneer. "They call it yellow journalism because everyone knows it's not the truth."

That remark, along with his mother's disapproval, set the tone for the entire miserable visit. I looked at my father.

"Are you kidding me?!" was the gist of my expression.

My father looked down for a moment. He knew that this was not the right way to start a conversation with me or anyone else. After a few more awkward interactions, it was suggested that the son and I go upstairs to have a conversation.

"You want a conversation?" I thought. "I'll give you a conversation." We went upstairs to the study, and I began my counteroffensive.

"Do you want to have children?" he asked.

"Oh yes, but not until I start my career," I answered.

"And then will you quit your career?" he replied.

"Oh no," I responded. "I don't want to be a stay-at-home mom."

"Who will take care of the children?" he asked, alarmed.

"I would just put them in daycare," I answered, innocently.

Bull's-eye. He was shocked. How could I do such a thing?! There had been a slew of daycare scandals reported in the '80s and early '90s (which shouldn't have bothered him, since he thought the news wasn't true). It looked like what I said did the trick. Then, just to make sure that I was thoroughly out of the running, I mentioned a friend's brother who had gone to the same school that he had. His facial expression soured. Not surprisingly, he didn't hold this person in a very high opinion.

"Oh, I think he's great!" I gushed. "I'm great friends with him." Much to my satisfaction, it went downhill from there.

The next morning, I went to the obligatory brunch and sat as far from the dour mother and son as possible. My pasted-on smile was beginning to fade as the conversation faltered and the uncomfortable silences grew. Between my father's naturally quiet nature, my mother's discomfort at being judged, and my disdain for the whole thing, the time couldn't have passed more slowly. After brunch, we said our goodbyes, and my father drove them to the airport.

For the next two months, my mother waited in anticipation but didn't hear anything. Finally, her network reported that the mother thought that my mother was a fast and loose woman. I thought that was hilarious, but my mother fumed. How dare this woman say that about her? It didn't seem to bother her that the woman had called me that too. But who cares? I dodged a bullet—at least for the moment.

CHAPTER THIRTEEN

OTHER THAN AVOIDING BEING married against my will, my days were spent scanning the New York Times classifieds for jobs, taking a typing class, and trying to figure out what to do. It seemed like the only jobs available were secretarial, and that's not why I went to NYU. I quit my typing class and grabbed the Staten Island newspaper, thinking that maybe I could find something locally. I was desperate.

Soon, I found an ad for a part-time newsletter writer. I was thrilled! Not only was this in my field, but it could also be a good starting point until I found something more appealing. I looked a little closer at the ad and saw that it was for a hospital on Staten Island. Was there no escape? I wanted to forge my own path, away from my father's reputation, even though it was a stellar one. Fortunately, I was relieved to see the job was at a hospital where no one would know me. I wouldn't be Dr. Bari's daughter. I would be judged on my own merits and abilities. I applied for the position and got it.

By the end of my first week on the job, I was given my first assignment: Interview the CEO of the new multisite hospital system. I figured if I could interview the founder of the Body Shop, I could do this. I drove to the administrative office and waited patiently in reception, where I couldn't help but notice how most of the people who worked there were either older white men or the stereotypical-looking secretaries who served them. I was glad I quit my typing class to aim higher.

Soon, a man sat next to me and started chatting me up. He asked me about my work, what I thought about my department, and what could be improved. I assumed he had an appointment as well, and answered honestly and politely. He nodded and listened—and then pointed to an office and told me to go in.

"I'm waiting for the CEO," I said.

"That's okay. I'll tell him you're here," he responded.

I walked into the office and took a seat in front of a large desk. A few seconds later, much to my surprise, the man I had just been talking to strolled in and sat behind the desk. He was the new CEO. The interview seemed to go well enough, and when I returned to the office, my boss greeted me with the news that the CEO, Rick, had just called.

"He wants us to hire you full-time," he said. "We're creating your job description."

I was shocked and elated. After I realized that the man that I had been talking to was actually the CEO, I had assured myself that I had done the right thing by following my instincts and answering him truthfully. He had appreciated it, and now I was being rewarded for trusting myself and *being* myself. It felt great. I was hired as a full-time communications specialist at a yearly salary of $27,000 plus benefits. That was double what I would have earned as an entry-level newscaster. I was working in my field and on my way to building the life of my dreams.

When I told my dad the news, I could tell he was proud of me, even if he didn't say it. The subject of work was where he and I connected best. It wasn't emotional, but it was meaningful. I didn't bother sharing much with my mother because she didn't understand and refused to show any pride in my accomplishments. Whatever I did, it was either not enough or not the right thing. Her response was always, "When are you getting married?" I learned to save work updates and accomplishments for my dad.

Living at home allowed me to save money so I could eventually move out for good. Since I didn't want to rely on my parents, I paid for a separate phone line, contributed to the groceries, bought my first car, and took care of all my expenses. I also researched financial literacy, opened my first retirement account, and established a savings plan. I'm not sure I could have tolerated being under the same roof as my mother again without doing these things. They were like a lifeline.

I went to work during the day and filled my nights with thoughts about what would be next. Once again, I was in my childhood bedroom dreaming of creating my future. That future did include a husband and children, but for now, I was more interested in using my skills, talents, and abilities to do work that I loved and that was meaningful to the world around me. This would be the foundation for my life. This would give me freedom financially, but also emotionally and psychologically.

After about six months on the job, I decided to apply to grad school, since the hospital offered tuition assistance. There was only one question: What should I study? Given my upbringing, medical school was always at the back of my mind. Even so, I quickly dismissed it. It wasn't for me even if my parents had wished it for me and pushed it on me from a young age. This was my life, and I wanted to live it my way. Next, I considered law school. I talked to a number of friends who had taken the LSAT more than once and tanked it. Since I didn't perform well on standardized tests, I thought the better of it.

I considered a master's in public health but realized I didn't really want to work in public policy or academia. I wanted the excitement that I experienced working on Park Avenue while also doing something that would help people. I briefly considered getting an MBA but doubted myself. Did I have the mind for it? I wasn't sure. Perhaps if I had seen women business leaders who looked like me, I wouldn't have thought twice. Instead, I decided to pursue a master's degree in arts at NYU, all paid for by the hospital. For the next three years, I worked full-time, drove into the city two nights a week for classes, and stayed in my room all day every Sunday studying. All my energy was focused on building a future I would be proud of.

My job at the hospital offered me a great deal of freedom and flexibility. Before long I was handling everything having to do with hospital communications, whether it was writing press releases, creating marketing brochures, or promoting community events. The department grew, and my position expanded. I directed my attention toward whatever new opportunities for growth I could find. Soon, one appeared.

Centers for Excellence was a term that hospitals were just beginning to use, and our hospital was no different. We had founded a new Center for Excellence for a radiation therapy used to treat tumors of the brain. Our physician was one of the very few in the New York tri-state area who did this procedure, and since the healthcare landscape is very competitive, I set about trying to figure out a way to reach more people so that they could learn about this powerful (and lucrative) new treatment that we offered. How could I make our Center for Excellence stand out and, in so doing, potentially save lives?

In terms of marketing, radio was considered a dead medium—especially with the advent of cable TV. If you brought it up, people would laugh. It was a waste of time and money. However, I thought otherwise. After all, since I had grown up driving with a dad who always listened to 1010 WINS, I knew there was a captive audience there—especially since the commuter audience was large and growing. Advertising on cable had its merits, but people needed to be sitting in front of the television. With radio, people just needed to be sitting in traffic, and there was always traffic in the New York Tri-state area. These are the people we need to reach, I thought.

I booked some spots on the local CBS radio station, wrote scripts, and set up a toll-free telephone line that went directly to the center's office, where they hired someone to receive the calls and follow a script that I also wrote for them. As soon as the spots were aired, the center was overwhelmed with calls. It became a huge success. Patients were getting the treatment they needed, and the hospital could continue to grow due to this lucrative new business. No longer was radio considered a "dead medium." Pretty soon, every hospital in the Tri-state area was advertising on radio. This affirmed for me again that I could trust myself. Just as I wouldn't blindly accept whatever the nuns or my mother told me, I wasn't going to blindly accept the belief about advertising on the radio. I reflected on my personal experience and thought otherwise, and it paid off.

I guess it shouldn't be a surprise that I refuse to blindly accept it the minute someone says, "That's just the way it is," or "That's how we've always done it." If I had done that growing up with my mother, I wouldn't be who I am today. I had to reject the status quo of my family—particularly of my mother—to survive. I wasn't going to accept her view of the world, of women, or who I should be. I wasn't going to submit. I wanted to be myself and make things happen, instead of just "phoning it in." If there's a better way to do something, I'm going to do it—which is how I ended up meeting Marilyn Quayle, the wife of then-Vice President Dan Quayle. All it took was an idea and courage—and I was motivated because the cause was such a worthy one.

We were planning a ribbon-cutting ceremony for the very first off-site ambulatory oncology unit approved by the New York Department of Health, which would make cancer treatment more accessible for patients. I thought this needed to be a truly special event, but ribbon ceremonies were sort of perfunctory. There was nothing particularly special about them. We needed to do something different. Thoughts started percolating in my mind.

During this time, Marilyn Quayle had been speaking publicly about losing her mother to breast cancer and had given emotional testimony to a congressional committee reviewing legislation to help uninsured women pay for mammograms and Pap smears. I thought how powerful it would be to have the second lady speak at the ribbon-cutting ceremony and decided to invite her. It was a long shot, and I wasn't even sure that her office would take the request seriously, but I knew that it couldn't hurt to try. They told me to submit a formal request, which I did, and, before I knew it, I had received my answer. She agreed! We were going to host the second lady of the United States. I was thrilled about what her attendance would mean for the opening and proud that I hadn't second-guessed my impulse to make the call. I knew that the worst thing that could have happened was that they'd say no. It's always worth the ask.

The next thing I knew, I was talking to the Secret Service about logistics, including possible escape routes in case something went wrong. I was only twenty-two years old, and this was heady stuff, but, again, it felt natural to me. It was like I had this inner knowing that said, "Of course, this is what I'm doing. Of course, we're hosting the second lady!" It was the same inner knowing that rebelled against my mother's ideas of who I was supposed to be in the world and whether or not the world would accept me. So far, I was doing fine. In fact, I was doing better than fine. The only person having a hard time accepting me was my mother.

My efforts securing Marilyn Quayle for the ribbon-cutting ceremony garnered us national attention, and Mrs. Quayle even wrote me a personal letter thanking me. I have it framed in my office to this day. I saw how powerful it was to trust my instincts and create connections to important figures and elected officials, and that by doing so, we could help people get the treatment that they needed and deserved. I was hungry for more—and I got it.

My role and responsibilities continued to expand, and I was essentially on-call 24/7 while also juggling my master's degree coursework. My beeper went off so frequently that I was tempted to throw it out the window. If a news story was developing that involved the hospital, I was the one the newspapers would call. Media relations was my least favorite part of the job, but I loved being a liaison between the community and our local officials. I loved being able to attract attention to the important programs we were offering. When the hospital's chief of staff wanted to start a new residency, I was the one he'd call. If a department was doing clinical trials, it was my phone that would ring. If someone wanted to start a support group, they would come to me. Everyone from community boards to pharmaceutical companies would reach out to me. If it involved the hospital, it involved me. It wasn't long before my name was constantly being paged over the loudspeaker—just as I had heard my father's when I was growing up. My father was interested in the work I was doing, and I loved sharing it with him. My mother, on the other hand, would just shake her head as if my work or accomplishments were shameful. I tried to ignore her and focused on my work, knowing that it was my key to independence.

My mantra became "I'm always where I need to be," and it's a philosophy I use to this day. If there were many conflicting priorities, I'd ask myself, "Where is my time best spent?" This approach would pay off later in my career as things became more demanding and complicated than I ever could have imagined.

I was doing good work and wanted to keep growing professionally, but when it came to further advancement, hospitals, like many organizations, are very political and tend toward the old boy network that is primarily white. Success was more about who you knew within the organization and community rather than what you actually accomplished. In fact, during my time at the hospital, we only had one female executive, and I rarely interacted with her.

To rise through the ranks in the hospital, someone had to either die or retire, and often they were replaced by someone who looked just like them and went to the same schools and country clubs. I knew I didn't want to be at the hospital forever, but I still wanted to be afforded the opportunity for growth. This could have been an "I told you so" moment for my mother, who never believed I'd never be accepted or supported. However, the one person who did support me during this time was my boss, a white man who wanted to see me grow and gave me ample room to do so.

Joseph was the father of four daughters who were about my age, and he became somewhat of a surrogate father to me. We'd work long hours, talk strategy, and grab meals together. Joseph's support was particularly helpful after his new boss was appointed. Because of his previous career in local politics, Joseph's new boss was used to being a big fish in a small pond. His behavior around young women also was known to be inappropriate. It wasn't long before he turned his attention in my direction and asked me out to lunch. Since it was only lunch and I didn't feel like I could say no, I went.

Instead of choosing a local spot, he chose a restaurant in New Jersey. When I arrived, we were ushered into a horseshoe-shaped booth. I was polite and professional and relieved that the only thing I had to deal with was the occasional weird look from him, but, as we were getting up to leave, he suddenly leaned over and kissed my cheek. I'm not sure if he was going for my mouth, because I reflexively turned my face away, but I felt like throwing up.

"I enjoyed getting to know you better," he said suggestively. "You're a very bright young woman with a bright future ahead of you." The subtext was that he could help me with my bright future. He suggested that we go out again, but I just played dumb. This was decades ahead of the #MeToo movement and, like many women, I learned how to navigate around these types of men and situations. Having allies helped, and, luckily, my boss was one of them.

When I got back to the office, I told Joseph what happened, and he did his best to minimize his boss's direct contact with me whenever he could. Unfortunately, there was nothing he could do when the letch asked me to help raise money for the hospital's charity ball. He had a department at his disposal precisely created to do fundraising, but he wanted me, and he wanted me specifically so that he could exploit the connections I had built within the community and among physicians, as well as take advantage of my father's good name. This made me deeply uncomfortable. I'm good at a lot of things, but leveraging my relationships and creating a quid pro quo is not something I am comfortable with from an integrity standpoint. I made a few calls, but it felt so inappropriate that I stopped and told him to look elsewhere. I wanted as little to do with him as possible.

CHAPTER FOURTEEN

IT WAS TIME TO move out of my parents' house. I just couldn't come home from work and stay in my high school bedroom any longer. The white lacquer furniture was finally getting to me, as was living under my mother's oppressive roof. Every interaction with her caused me anxiety or frustration—so much so that I thought it was normal. Fortunately, I had saved some money and, after subscribing to Kiplinger's Personal Finance newsletter, I was even investing some of it. Looking at my bank account, I realized that I could actually afford to buy my own place—and I wasn't even twenty-five years old! I looked at the real estate listings in the newspaper, knowing that I didn't want to live on Staten Island but that I had to be close enough to commute to my job even if I wasn't going to be there more than a few years. My weekends were spent driving to various communities, and soon I found a beautiful two-bedroom condo in Parlin, New Jersey, just over the bridge from Staten Island. Plus, it was also close to Lisa's new home in Middletown, where she lived with her husband and two boys.

After looking at similar condominiums in the area and comparing prices, I reached out to the realtor and put in an offer. The property was listed under a hundred thousand. Because I had done my research, my offer was low, which I knew would give us somewhere to go with the negotiations. I was also prepared to walk away if I had to. The realtor came back with ninety-nine thousand. I came back with eighty-nine thousand. She came back with a higher price, which I countered with an even lower offer.

"I'll offer you eighty-five thousand," I said.

She balked. I knew the market and, even though the condo was a desirable corner unit, certain features hadn't been upgraded. I made my case and quickly learned that I was innately good at negotiating. This was different from my mother, who would haggle about everything just to be cheap. I didn't want to be cheap. I just wanted to be fair and base my offer on the facts, and if it didn't work out, I wasn't afraid to walk away, which I did. And then I waited. In no time, the phone rang.

"I don't know how you did it," the realtor said. The owner had agreed to come down fifteen thousand dollars from her list price to match my offer. The condo was finally mine! At a mere twenty-three years old, I was a first-time homeowner. The experience was extremely validating. My instincts were spot on, and since they were based on the research I had done, it didn't completely surprise me. This approach of supporting my instincts with facts, data, and research would continue to serve me well—not only in buying houses but in navigating career successes, as well.

Once again, I told my dad after the fact.

"That's a great investment," he said, thinking I was just going to rent it out.

"Oh no, I'm going to live there," I explained.

He looked at me, shocked. "Young, unmarried Muslim women don't live alone!" he said. "That's completely inappropriate. What will people think?"

His response didn't surprise me, but it's not like we were living in 1892. It was 1992, and unmarried Western women were definitely living alone and doing a whole lot more. In fact, 1992 was labeled the Year of the Woman after more women were voted into the United States Senate than decades prior—due in large part to Anita Hill's treatment after testifying against Supreme Court nominee Clarence Thomas for sexual harassment. The Year of the Woman was preceded by the landmark feminist film *Thelma & Louise* which garnered six Academy Award nominations and, in the years to follow, the phrase "girl power" would become a pop culture phenomenon thanks to feminist punk bands like Bikini Kill. This was the zeitgeist, but my parents were living in another era and referencing another culture and another world. This was exactly what I was trying to get away from.

Regardless, my dad knew me well enough that he realized, when it came down to it, I was going to do what I was going to do. After a few days of awkward silence, our relationship returned to normal. Ultimately, he trusted my judgment, and I knew that—even if he didn't say it outright. I furnished the condo modestly, and, just like when I went to college, I took only my personal belongings and clothing from my parents' house.

When it came time for them to visit, I could sense their pride as they saw how nice the condo was with its outdoor deck, high vaulted ceilings, and windows that looked out onto the woods next door. My mother gave me a vacuum cleaner and some dishes as a housewarming present and, after they left, I closed the door and felt a momentary sense of peace.

CHAPTER FIFTEEN

WHEN I GOT THE job at the hospital, I started crafting my twenty-year career plan. Just like when I was younger, I would tuck myself in my twin bed and envision the life I wanted to create. Now that I was older (but still in my high school twin bed), I got specific.

Buy my own home. Done.

Move out of my parents' house. Done.

Next, I planned on staying at the hospital for no more than three to five years, after which I wanted to get a job at one of the top PR agencies in New York City, one that had accounts with the leading global healthcare companies. After getting agency experience, my goal was to work in-house at one of the top two.

Exciting things were happening in healthcare, and I wanted to be a part of it. During the late '80s, the first anti-depressant hit the market, which changed the conversation around mental health—so much so that it made the cover of *Time* magazine in 1992. That same year, the first gene linked to inherited early-onset Alzheimer's disease was discovered. I didn't know then that both of those discoveries would figure prominently in my own life, but I knew that I wanted to be part of solutions that could change people's lives for the better, just like I saw my dad doing. But ultimately, I wanted to be my own boss doing something involving healthcare and communications, but, from my current vantage point at my first professional job, I wasn't exactly sure what that would be. Nevertheless, I had my twenty-year plan, and it was time to make a move.

The first thing I did was reach out to a sorority sister from NYU and mention that I wanted to break into the agency world. As luck would have it, she had a friend from law school whose sister had a big role at one of the agencies.

"Let me talk to her," she said.

Within no time, I had an interview. Regardless of my previous successes at the hospital, I had no real agency experience apart from my internship in college, and even though I had experience working with executives, physicians, and local politicians, I didn't have any experience working with the type of corporate clients that agencies cater to. In order for them to take me seriously, I would need to convince them that I was worth taking on.

On the day of the interview, I brought a portfolio that I had made with all the marketing and communication materials I had created during my time at the hospital. I wanted them to see the quality, quantity, and diversity of output that I had generated. Did they ask me to bring this? No. But I knew I had to show them what I was capable of. The years of living under my mother's roof with her constant quips that I would never be good enough haunted me. I knew she was wrong and I was going to prove it.

Even though I wanted the job, I was clear that I specifically wanted to work in the kind of healthcare that saved people's lives. Similar to when I bought the house, the subtext was that I was willing to walk away. I got the job. When I told my dad, he sent me flowers.

My first experiences working at an agency might have been different if the person who had hired me had become my boss. Unfortunately, she wasn't. Instead, she was in a senior position over my boss, who was a VP and nothing short of brutal. The evil boss in *Working Girl* was nothing compared to her. She made Miranda Priestly in *The Devil Wears Prada* look like a pussycat. Almost every day, I was called into her office and yelled at. Everything I did was wrong and everything I wrote was crossed out with her blood-red pen without any explanation. Sometimes, she'd just rip up my work right in front of me. Instead of telling me why or doing any form of mentoring, she micromanaged the life out of me.

"Maybe we shouldn't have hired you," she snarled. I started to doubt myself and my abilities.

"Are you stupid?!" she yelled one day. "ARE YOU ABSO-LUTELY STUPID?"

The only good thing about having a mother who constantly tries to degrade you is that it somewhat prepares you for people like this. My day-to-day life was hell, but I had years of practice not showing that the abusive behavior was getting to me. When my colleagues cried in their cubicles on a regular basis, I coped by getting very quiet. It's not like I could talk back to her like I could talk back to my mother, and I certainly wasn't going to go to HR about it. The whole environment was dysfunctional and toxic—words that barely existed to describe workplaces back then.

It may have been called the Year of the Woman in Congress but, to put it in perspective, there were only 54 women in Congress, out of 535 members (and let's not forget that the triumphant ending of *Thelma & Louise* was that they drove off a cliff). Yet the person who was my biggest obstacle was my female boss—not a man. She'd laugh and joke with the other female VPs, but, with me, she behaved completely the opposite. She had their ear, and whatever she was saying about me was not good. To say there wasn't a culture of female mentorship in the '90s (and on into the aughts) would be an understatement. There just weren't the programs or mandates to support it. Women were focused on advancing their careers and surviving in a male-dominated workforce, and if you couldn't handle it, then get the hell out—and quick.

I knew I wasn't happy, but I wasn't about to quit regardless of the battering my confidence was receiving. I had my twenty-year plan to think of. Every morning, I would take the train from New Jersey to Penn Station and join the fast-moving mob of commuters making their way to work. At the end of the day, it was the same in reverse. One rainy morning, I was on the train surrounded by middle-aged men wearing trench coats, reading the paper in silence.

"I'm too young for this," I thought.

I looked forward to weekends and weeknights, which were mostly spent with Lisa and her kids and husband. I loved it there. It was family, and it was easy and safe. I never wanted to go out and do anything like I did in college. I didn't really know anyone in Manhattan, anyway, and I certainly wasn't going to hang out on Staten Island.

One day, Lisa took me aside. "You have to move into the

city," she said. "You're young and single and you're living in suburbia. You have to get out."

She was right. Something had to change. It's not like things could get worse—until they did.

A couple of months into working at the agency, I was at my parents' house moving some of my belongings into my car. I bent down to pick up a box and felt a tweak in my back. I didn't think much of it and kept going. The following week, I took the train to work and was at the bottom of the subway station stairs when my legs stopped working. I used every ounce of my willpower to force them to move, but it was like I was paralyzed. Nothing happened. I leaned against the railing in excruciating pain and pulled myself up the stairs with my arms. By the time I got to my office, I crumbled to the floor in tears.

"What's wrong?" my coworker asked.

"My back," I whispered through the tears and searing pain.

The doctor told me that I had herniated a couple of discs. I had never had back problems before. Did it have to do with being yelled at and belittled by my boss on a daily basis? Did it have to do with that behavior being similar to how I was treated by my mother when I was growing up? Studies have shown a link between chronic pain, PTSD, and trauma, but all I knew at the time was that I could barely move and that the doctor was prescribing bed rest. This meant only one thing. I had to move back home with my parents.

Everything I had done to become independent of my parents quickly slipped from my grasp. I couldn't tie my shoes by myself. I couldn't go to the bathroom by myself, and I could barely sneeze without convulsing in pain. Instead, I had to rely on my dad and mother for my care—especially my mother, since my father worked during the day. My mind flooded with anxiety about my job. Would I be fired from my very first agency job? I was afraid that my boss would use this leave of absence against me, and if I lost my job, how would I pay my mortgage? How would it look on my resume? I felt completely powerless.

I ended up being on medical disability for four and a half months. The day I came back, I wasn't sure what to expect. I braced myself, walked into my office, and found someone else sitting there. She had been hired in my absence.

"Hi, I'm Stephanie," said the woman. "I'm going to be sharing your office."

I breathed a sigh of relief. I thought she was my replacement. I put my things down and assessed the situation. Would we be competitors or colleagues? I hoped for the latter. Little did I know that we would become close friends. A few moments later, a man walked in and introduced himself as Paul. He was a VP, just like my boss, and had advocated for me while my boss tried to spread disparaging rumors about me among the senior management.

"You haven't even given her a chance," he had told them. "Let me work with her."

He became the second man in my career to advocate for me. Instead of chastising me, he encouraged dialogue and let me think things through. Instead of trying to survive in a tense and toxic environment, we would laugh and have fun. Instead of trying to squash me, he'd let me grow. I quickly began to flourish. It was a huge learning experience.

Prior to Paul, I had been torturing myself trying to figure out what I was doing wrong and how I had gone from doing so well at the hospital to doing so poorly here. I couldn't make sense of it. And then I did. It wasn't a talent problem. It was a personal problem, and the person was my boss. If I learned anything from that experience, it was how not to be—as a leader or just a human being.

Working with Paul restored my sanity and sense of self. I wasn't going to let people walk all over me anymore. This came in handy many times. For example, there was another female leader who was notorious for being cold and rude. She was the kind of person who wouldn't acknowledge you if you got on an elevator with her. She never smiled or even looked at me. She belonged to the group of women VPs who clawed their way to the top and weren't interested in helping other women. If anything, it seemed like they were more interested in constantly testing you to see if you'd break. I refused to break and, knowing that I had an ally in Paul, I could stand in my strength, which I did, much to her surprise.

At the time, we were hiring new staff, and she hired someone I didn't think was a good fit. When that person predictably didn't work out, she tried to put her on my team.

"You're the one who hired her," I said. "You keep her." The woman looked at me impressed and a little shocked.

"Oh my gosh," she exclaimed. "She's finally found her voice!" I passed the test. Unfortunately, there would be more to come. Next, came the client from hell—or at least that's what he was called in the office. No one wanted to work with him, and he didn't like any of our teams. He had been passed around from person to person within the agency until, finally, his company's portfolio of products landed on Paul's desk since he was the newest VP. This client was used to bullying our junior staff, who were, of course, mostly women. One day, it was my turn.

I picked up the phone, and before I knew it, he started screaming about something. He was going on and on until finally I interrupted and said, "Wow, you're really upset. Why don't we talk in a little bit?" And then, without waiting for his response, I calmly hung up the phone.

I sat at my desk, feeling a slight fluttering in my chest. This account was worth millions of dollars. Did I do the right thing? A few moments later, the phone rang. I knew it was him. I took a breath and picked up the phone. He was laughing.

"No one has ever done that to me," he said. "But wow, is that effective! I'm calm now so let's talk."

I felt invigorated. I had stood up for myself and again, it had paid off. This had never happened when I was with my mother. Growing up, I would stand up for myself, but she never heard me. I never earned her respect. This was a decidedly different experience, and it fueled me. I became the client's go-to person and was able to flex my decision-making muscles when things went well and when things went not so well—which is exactly what happened one evening in New Orleans.

I had been working with this client, who was going to launch a new medicine at the premier pain science conference attended by hundreds of esteemed researchers and physicians from around the country. This is not a place where you want to blow it.

After working months preparing for this multi-million-dollar launch, I walked into the conference hall as the opening night ceremonies were about to begin, but the client was nowhere to be found. Where were they? Frantically, I called everyone on their team, but no one answered. This was no way to launch a potentially revolutionary new medicine. I decided to take matters into my own hands. In retrospect, this was a useful survival strategy that came from childhood. Growing up, if there was a problem at home, my mother was useless, and my dad would come to me instead. They also couldn't help me navigate being an American kid or teenager, I had to navigate that on my own, as well. I had come to rely on myself, and more importantly, to trust myself and my instincts since I couldn't trust my mother to support me or keep me safe. I was beginning to see how my instincts were paying off professionally.

I decided the best thing I could do was stand in for the client, open their conference booth. I even accepted an award on their behalf and had my picture taken for the newspaper. When it was all over, I returned to my hotel, wondering if I was going to get fired. It was a long, sleepless night.

I didn't get fired. I found out the next day that they had gotten the opening ceremony date wrong and were grateful for what I had done. The next time I walked into the client's headquarters for a meeting, I received a standing ovation. The words of my mother rang in my head: "They will never accept you." I looked around the room and wondered what she would think if she could see me now.

CHAPTER SIXTEEN

MARK TWAIN SAID THAT the difference between the right word and almost the right word is the difference between lightning and a lightning bug. I guess it should be no surprise that choosing the right word, or the right image, became so important to me. No matter how hard I tried to communicate with my mother, she refused to hear me, regardless of the endless strategies I tried. When it came to my work, I wasn't about to let this happen—especially working with a client that had just developed the first oral medicine for metastatic breast cancer. The incidence of breast cancer had risen by over fifty percent since the 1950s, and this medicine would target only the tumor instead of the healthy tissue surrounding it. I reached out to *CBS Evening News* and invited them to interview the medical director. They agreed. Knowing that TV is a visual medium, I wanted to inspire the graphics people at the network to create images that would capture people's attention. I likened the medicine to a heat-seeking missile that would strategically target and destroy the tumor. The segment was a success.

I remember my dad saying that he didn't want to pay for my degree in journalism, which is essentially communications. He thought it was frivolous because, in his community, you were either a doctor, a lawyer, or an architect. My parents acted like they had never even heard of journalism as a major, but now I was making my living from it and doing it at a healthcare agency.

~

My twenty-year plan was proceeding nicely. I found myself working more and more with top leaders and executives, and it felt good. I was comfortable talking to doctors and healthcare leaders. Perhaps this was due to my earlier experience interning at the hospital or going to medical conferences with my dad during college. Perhaps it was because I wanted to help people and I wanted to work with people who were doing just that. I wasn't about to let anyone fail.

Because of that, the client whom I had calmly hung up on came to me instead of the senior executive when it was time to resign his business from the agency. He trusted me. I had become his go-to person.

"How dare he not come to me first?!" the senior executive asked incredulously. It was a small moment of satisfaction after all the belittling and toxic behavior that the senior VPs had engaged in.

Could this have happened if I had stayed working under the boss who only wanted to tear me down? Definitely not. It was possible because Paul believed in me and gave me ample room to grow. This is the mark of a true manager, leader, and mentor. Never settle for anything less and don't let anyone tear down your belief in yourself.

Back then, today's conversation around work/life balance was practically nonexistent, and my life became consumed with work. I'd work long days and nights, take the train back to New Jersey, and arrive past midnight, only to get back on the train at 6 the next morning. My dating and social life was nonexistent. It was time to take Lisa's advice and move out of the 'burbs.

Manhattan seemed overwhelming, so I rented out my condo in New Jersey and found a ground-floor garden apartment in a four-unit brownstone in Park Slope, Brooklyn, which was a quick train or taxi ride from the city. Now I could go out after work. My relationship with both Stephanie and Paul grew, and soon we were sharing work lunches, dinners, or late-night drinks.

Paul, who was gay, became my plus-one at many events and visits with my parents. Even though I was beginning to date here and there, nothing felt serious enough to warrant a parental introduction. My parents became completely enamored with Paul, which surprised me since my mother was such a bigot, but I think they felt safe with him. He was delightful and charming and won them over easily.

Soon, my weekends became full of mimosa brunches, window shopping, and hanging out with Stephanie. Even if my mother couldn't be proud of me, I was. I was making a good salary and could pay the mortgage on my condo in New Jersey, rent an apartment in Park Slope, and still have money to go out to dinners and take taxis home. Since I was continuing to financially educate myself, I made sure to fully fund my 401(k) at work and continue saving. I couldn't talk to my dad about money because, though he was a great doctor, he didn't have a head for finances. As with most things, I had to rely on myself. After a couple of years, I was finally ready to move to Manhattan.

You'd never know from watching *Friends* or *Sex and the City* how hard it is to find a great affordable place in New York City, but real estate in the '90s was cutthroat. If you found an apartment listed, you'd have to get up at the crack of dawn to be the first person in line to see it. Then you'd have to carry the cash deposit with you, which didn't feel very safe, but would give you the competitive edge if you were lucky enough to get it. If you didn't, the apartment might go to the person behind you. It was a little daunting, but I was committed.

When Paul mentioned that apartments were becoming available in his Madison Avenue building, I jumped on it. He introduced me to the building manager whose family owned most of the apartments. For the next few weeks, I would visit regularly just so they wouldn't forget about me. Finally, an apartment became available on the same floor as Paul's, and I made the move. I loved living in the building, having friends nearby, and told the landlord that I wanted to buy it if it ever became available.

Having my own apartment in the city was a dream come true. I'd go over to Paul's for a drink or coffee, and we'd chat about work and life. Even though he had his circle of friends, and I had mine, it was nice to have a friend who lived so close. Stephanie and I were also spending more and more time together. We'd go to events at places like the world-famous Tavern on the Green in Central Park or the Intrepid on the Hudson River. After work on Fridays, we'd usually stop by our favorite bar, Rare, in Murray Hill and order their lamb burgers. It was always packed. On weekends, there was more window shopping on Fifth Avenue or escapes to her beach house in Avalon, New Jersey.

Stephanie, like Lisa, was becoming something of a sister to me, and that relationship would only grow. She even got an apartment in my building for a couple of years. Through her, my friend circle expanded into what I had been looking for when I joined the sorority back at NYU. She introduced me to her friends from college, Carrie, Andrea, and Linda. We used to joke that our lives were like *Sex and the City* even though we didn't really watch it. Our sentiment was basically "We don't have to watch it. We're too busy living it." We were in our twenties, had disposable income, and the freedom to do what we wanted with it. My twenty-year plan was meeting my expectations, and it was more fun and fulfilling than I could have imagined.

Soon Paul left the agency to take a new position as the head of another agency's global healthcare practice. He asked me to come with him, and I couldn't wait. I joined the company as a VP, but I would be nothing like the female VP I had worked under. I was finally coming into my own and knew that I was capable of more. My relationship with my dad only grew during these years, as we now had more and more to talk about. My mother, of course, thought I was ruining my life and, more to the point, ruining hers—or at least her reputation within her community.

Working with Paul at my second agency continued to be rewarding. He never asked me to play smaller or hide what I thought. Soon, there was a piece of business that needed to be pitched to a potential new client. When our team went into the meeting, the client asked each of us for our opinion. Normally, the senior person goes first, and then everyone else basically repeats the same thing. That was the drill. This time, after the senior VP went, I didn't just repeat what he said. I gave my honest opinion, because it's what I thought would serve the client better. Again, I trusted myself, deciding that integrity was more important than "phoning it in." Everyone who went after me followed suit, and the client was impressed by our intellectual rigor and independent thinking. This was a far cry from being whacked on the knuckles by the nuns in Catholic school. We won the account.

Later, when the company was running clinical trials, they mentioned to Paul that the interim results were very positive. This was great news, but I also realized that if the data was showing that the medication was working, the company would be ethically bound to stop the trial. You can't have people on a placebo if you have something that will help them.

"You're right," agreed Paul.

He called the company back, and after a discussion with the drug safety board, they stopped the trial early. My job at the agency was in communications and thinking this way was not part of the role, but I have never been defined by a role. I have always been drawn to the bigger picture. If I had accepted my role as a Muslim girl, I wouldn't be where I found myself—building the life of my dreams. Seeing the bigger picture was another survival strategy that was paying off professionally. From that point on, they gave me a seat at the table for all their strategic decisions. I went on to manage the launch of that new product, and it quickly became a multibillion-dollar medicine treating a condition that causes pain to so many.

Before long, black limos were lining up outside the client's headquarters as larger companies were beginning to court this lucrative company. They were bought by a company that I wanted to work for someday. It was one of the top two on my twenty-year plan, but, for now, that would have to wait.

As good as these professional successes felt, I still struggled with anxiety, which would intensify every time I had to interact with my mother. Just the sound of her voice would cause my stomach to tighten. Instead of feeling like the successful grown-ass woman that I was, I would be reminded of that little girl, still trapped in her ugly bedroom, burning inside with rage. I started going to therapy, hoping it would help me deal with the anxiety and my mother. My doctor put me on Prozac and gave me a prescription for Xanax, which I would use when I had to see her. I hoped this would help.

CHAPTER SEVENTEEN

IF THINGS WITH MY mother hadn't changed, my life away from her would continue to. My landlord called to tell me that they were selling my apartment and ask if I wanted to buy it. He gave me a price, and I quickly agreed to it. Finally, I would own a home in New York City! I started getting the money together and filling out the mortgage application. Then, everything changed.

"I'm sorry, the apartment is actually worth more," he said.

"How much more?" I asked, not expecting him to quote me a hundred thousand more! I was floored.

"We've been talking about this for a long time," I countered. "It's pretty despicable to change everything at the last moment."

He felt guilty and finally agreed to sell me the apartment at the original price he had quoted me, which, in the end, turned out to be well under the market value. At the time, the neighborhood was full of empty lots and prostitution, but I knew that would eventually change. I sold my apartment in New Jersey for a small profit and settled into homeownership in one of the most exciting cities in the world. Little did I know I'd soon be moving far away.

~

I had always wanted to be my own boss, and suddenly, I was being given the opportunity. It was at a new agency, which was primarily based in New York but had a smaller office in Los Angeles that wasn't generating enough business to be viable. They wanted me to change that. I agreed on two conditions. I would do it only for a finite period of time, and, since I didn't want to give up my recently purchased apartment in the city and couldn't afford to pay another rent on top of my mortgage, they would have to cover my L.A. housing. They agreed and I started working with the CFO to create a business plan with revenue targets. I was itching to get started.

I flew into LAX in the middle of the night and picked up my rental car and the keys to my new, furnished apartment in Marina Del Rey. I had never been to L.A. and didn't know a soul, so beyond being a professional challenge, it was a personal one as well. The next morning, I woke up to the sound of sea lions barking in the harbor, grabbed the keys to my rental convertible sports car, and went to work, where I met Betty, the woman who had been running the office. I quickly went about hiring a team and drumming up new business. I soon found out that most of the healthcare companies weren't actually in Los Angeles but up north, in the San Francisco Bay Area. So, almost every week, I would take the short flight to Oakland to attend pitches and meetings in Palo Alto and other areas of the Peninsula. It was the beginning of the type of travel that would characterize my professional life, and then, unfortunately, my personal life, as well.

Out of the blue, I received a call that stopped me cold in my tracks. My father was diagnosed with renal failure. Without dialysis or a kidney transplant, he would survive only a few months. I was shocked, to say the least.

"Why didn't you take care of yourself?!" I asked him.

For years, he had been complaining that his sugar was high, and I would pester him to get it checked out. "If your sugar is high, it's diabetes," I'd say. "You need to get on medication." But, like most doctors, he was a lousy patient. He was more focused on his patients than taking care of himself, and now his kidneys were failing. He even decided to do dialysis at home instead of in the hospital because he didn't want to alarm his patients. I knew he needed me, even though he would never say it, and I knew that taking care of my dad also meant taking care of my mother.

It was frustrating that as much as I tried to free myself from her, I felt like I was constantly being pulled back into her toxic orbit. Now, I was three thousand miles away, in the middle of building a new business and being called home once again, but I knew I would go to any lengths for my father.

I booked my flight, and from that point on, every other weekend, I would fly back and forth between L.A. and New York to help him with his treatment and my mother with everything else. My dad wanted to do dialysis at home instead of at the hospital because he didn't want anyone to know about his condition. I needed to make sure that he and my mother knew what they were doing since I couldn't be there all the time.

On top of my father's care and building the West Coast office, I still had my clients in New York to take care of. One client asked me to accompany an important researcher by the name of Joseph Druker to the American Academy of Clinical Research annual meeting. Since my mantra is "I'm always where I need to be," I, of course, agreed. His research went on to revolutionize the treatment of cancer. By this time, it almost felt like I lived at the airport, but the work sustained me and, if anything, distracted me from worrying about my father. This was another survival strategy from childhood. As long as I stayed busy, I could avoid the reality at home, and more importantly, avoid feeling the painful emotions. I was nothing like my mother, who spent most of the day in bed. It was depressing to witness and the last thing I would ever do. If rage fueled me as a kid, keeping busy and working toward my twenty-year plan only added to that fuel. I was working seven days a week, but I loved being my own boss. I was also lonely.

Since I didn't know anyone in L.A., my nights would consist of stopping by Trader Joe's before they closed, going home to make something to eat, and watching TV before falling into bed. Sometimes I'd go to the gym. Occasionally, I was invited to parties where it seemed like everyone in L.A. worked in the entertainment industry or, at least, aspired to.

"What do you do?" they'd ask me.

"I work in PR," I'd say.

"Oh, really? Doing what?" they'd continue with great interest.

"Healthcare," I'd answer.

And that would be the end of that. They'd just turn and walk away, without even making an excuse. They couldn't have cared less. It was almost comical.

During the rare weekends when I was in town and not working, I'd drive up the coast to Malibu in my red Camaro. It wasn't that I loved Camaros in particular, but I figured if the agency was going to rent me a car, I might as well live a little. It was during one of these drives up the Pacific Coast Highway that I noticed a swarm of helicopters hovering over the mountains for a wedding—Jennifer Aniston and Brad Pitt's wedding. This was definitely different from taking the subway in New York.

Instead of trekking through the snow in a New York winter, I was sitting on the deck in my building's Jacuzzi in seventy-degree weather. My strolls down Fifth Avenue were replaced by strolls along the beach, over the Venice canals, past the original Gold's Gym (made famous by Arnold Schwarzenegger), and along the boardwalk to Muscle Beach, where the bodybuilders pumped iron in front of an audience of tourists. I'd continue down the bike path to the Santa Monica Pier, where I'd grab a lobster roll. All the time I spent alone in my room as a kid gave me the ability to enjoy my own company, and these days were no exception.

As I assembled my team at work, I didn't shy away from hiring the "underdog," meaning the person who might be overlooked. I often felt like the underdog at home, so I knew the drive and potential that could be uncovered. One time I hired someone no one else wanted to hire because she had only been an office manager at a dermatology office, but I took a chance on her, and she's a successful professional today. I hired another young woman who worked at a Blockbuster video rental store who is now a VP. Another time, I hired someone who was in a wheelchair, and everybody was worried about how the office would handle the logistics of that. Of course, it was not a problem, and she was a great hire, as I knew she would be.

Since I had grown up with a mom who was biased and judgmental about everyone, including me, I wasn't about to pass up talent because of small-minded thinking. Within eight months, I brought in $1.4 million worth of new business, exceeding our financial targets by 50 percent. It would soon be time to go back to NYC for good and hand over the reins to the team I had assembled and mentored. I proved to myself that I could be a boss and that I was as good as any guy—even though my mother said I would never be. I did it, and I wanted to do it again.

CHAPTER EIGHTEEN

"YOUR DAD'S HAVING TROUBLE breathing," my mother said. "He's in the hospital." I put down the phone and headed to the airport. My dad had been in Chicago on one of his Islamic Medical Association trips. When I arrived at the hospital, I was greeted by a team of residents.

"There's fluid around his heart and lungs," they said. "We think it might be congestive heart failure."

"That's ridiculous," I responded. "I'm sure it's a perforation from the dialysis."

They looked at me like I didn't know what I was talking about.

"Are you a physician?" countered the resident, dismissively.

"No, I just have common sense," I replied, frustrated.

I spent the night at the hospital and was sitting by my father's bed the next day when the resident who questioned me earlier walked in.

"You were right," he said. "I'm glad you said what you said."

That was the end of at-home dialysis. It was too risky. I reached out to the head of nephrology at the hospital and asked if my dad could receive dialysis at the hospital before the patients arrived. He would have his privacy while also being safe. Once that was arranged, I needed to get my father home from Chicago, but I couldn't go with him since I needed to be back at work in L.A. My mother was incapable of doing it. I coordinated with a trusted car service to meet my father at the airport with a wheelchair and help him into the house and his bed.

This is when I started becoming the decision-maker for issues concerning my father's health. I was the one they would rely on in a crisis, just as I was the one my clients would rely on in a crisis. No matter what was happening, I had the ability to shut off my emotions and focus on what needed to get done. If there was emotion to be had, I would express it later and alone. Being able to compartmentalize my emotions would be a highly rewarded skill in my professional life and helped me through the increasingly difficult times with my parents. I suppose it was partly because of them and how I was raised that I could do this.

Many families have unspoken covenants, and if my family had one, it was, "don't feel." The predominant emotion exhibited by my mother could today be described as depression, but, as a child growing up in the '70s, I didn't know that's what lying in bed all day meant. When I would tell my dad about it, he'd say, "She's okay. That's just how she is."

The first time I saw a tear fall from my father's eyes was when I was in my twenties. My mother's sister had recently died, and he was hugging one of her daughters. He didn't even cry when his brother died. He just got quiet. It wasn't until I was in my thirties that he finally said that he loved me. I knew that he did, but it felt good to hear it. My mother never said it. Instead, she would say, "my heart beats for you," or "I breathe for you," but it felt more suffocating and controlling than affectionate.

The one feeling I knew all too well was anxiety. I knew that talking to my mother was a trigger, along with my concerns about my father's health. Not only was I afraid of losing him, but I also knew that when I did, my mother would become my responsibility because she depended on him for everything. Even though I adored my father, I knew he had enabled this behavior. This was probably a reflection of his generation and culture. If I blamed my father for anything, it was for putting his patients' health before his own and fostering my mother's dependency.

With my dad taken care of and the office up and running in L.A., it was finally time to return to my home in New York City, where I would continue therapy hoping for the support I so desperately needed when it came to dealing with my mother. It would take a long time before I finally came to the decision that, ultimately, saved my life.

~

Back at the agency in New York, it didn't take long before I started feeling antsy. It was time for a new challenge. Around that time, Paul received an offer from another agency and, again, asked me to join him. Coincidentally, it was the same agency that had rejected me years earlier when I was a new NYU graduate, so it felt particularly gratifying, but I knew this was going to be my last agency. It was time for the next thing on my twenty-year plan and that was to work in-house at a global pharmaceutical company. I reached out to my recruiter network.

"Call me with something exciting," I told them. "Something in-house."

My personal life was full of friends and fun evenings and weekends. What a stark contrast to L.A.! On Saturday mornings, I would take golf lessons at the premier golf club in New York City, located at Chelsea Piers where the driving range looks out over the beautiful Hudson River. Three mornings a week, I would work out with my trainer at the neighborhood gym, and, after work, I would go take a yoga class to help me unwind. As driven as I am, it's not competition that drives me—unless it comes to competing against myself. I loved setting personal goals and then surpassing them. I wanted to be in the best physical shape I could be (especially after my back injury earlier in my career). I never wanted to be that helpless and dependent on anyone again. These activities centered me and, in many ways, were a form of meditation and mindfulness.

Psychologically, I was continuing to work in therapy on the issues with my mother and her narcissism. I started practicing boundaries by only being available for phone calls once a week at a predetermined time. My mother didn't like this and would nag my father about it or complain to me, particularly because she knew I often talked to my dad. It was always easier to talk to my dad. We bonded over work and so this was what our conversations were about. They weren't deep or personal, but I enjoyed them, and it gave me a sense of connection. The older I got, the closer my father and I became. For this, I was grateful. With my mother, it was more of the same: constant criticism and pressure.

"Why can't we talk at night when you're home from work?" she'd ask, since this was her favorite time to talk on the phone.

"I talk all day," I explained. "I just want to be quiet at night."

"But I don't know what's going on with you. You haven't been home," she'd continue. Then she'd tell me about someone in her community whose daughter had just gotten married or had a baby.

"When are you going to get married?" she'd ask. "What are you waiting for?"

When I was in my early 20s, I dated a resident at the hospital, and, out of curiosity, I asked my mom if she would approve of me marrying a surgeon.

"Is he Muslim?" she asked.

"What if he's famous or superwealthy?" I continued. "Would you approve of him then?"

"It doesn't matter if he's not Muslim," she said. "He has to be Muslim."

That resident ended up becoming a famous Beverly Hills surgeon, but that wouldn't have been good enough for my mother, which is why I never brought anyone home. It's not like I had a problem finding dates, and I even did online dating in the days before swiping.

Once, Lisa set me up on a really bad date—so bad that I almost felt like jumping out of the restaurant's bathroom window to escape. The only reason I didn't was because he was Lisa's colleague.

"What's wrong with you?!" I asked her as we laughed until we cried about how awful it was. However, now that I was turning 30, I started noticing the engagement rings on women at work, at the gym, or on the train. But with all the pressure my mother put on me to find a "suitable" partner (meaning Muslim and not white), I wasn't emotionally available for a meaningful relationship. There was always the threat that I would be disowned from the family for picking a partner against my parent's wishes. Despite my disdain for my mother's views, the threat of being disowned created so much fear in me that I would inevitably sabotage what dating I did do. My mother was unrelenting.

When a son of one of my parents' friends married someone who wasn't Muslim, my mother said, "It's like a stone in his parents' hearts." I grew up hearing that, so I avoided relationships even if I knew that, deep down, I still had that little girl dream of marrying a handsome white man with green eyes and having adorable children with dimples.

In the meantime, I dove into my work, which gave me the opportunity to travel the world. That sounds glamorous but often wasn't. Even though I love experiencing different cultures and cuisines, there usually wasn't time. As a young professional, I was flying economy, and, even if the location was glamorous, the hotel wasn't. One time I was put in a shady motel in New Orleans, and I put a chair against the door just to be safe. Sometimes I'd have to entertain a client who wanted to go to a strip club, or they'd joke about the conference being by the beach so I should wear my bikini. (I didn't.) This behavior never came from the male executives. It was always middle management guys who were going nowhere. I didn't let it bother me, and it didn't influence how I acted. Some of the agency girls would drink with their clients, but I never did. I'd just order a club soda and pretend it was vodka soda.

Often my experience of different cultures and cuisines came from living in New York City, and with that exposure, I developed a love of fine wine. I decided to put my name on the waiting list for the world-renowned Windows on the World wine-tasting course located on the top floors of the World Trade Center. It took me six months until I finally got in. It was taught by the award-winning Kevin Zraly and his sommelier-in-training, Andrea Immer (now Robinson), who was named the best sommelier in the U.S. and is one of only a small group of women Master Sommeliers. My dream of rubbing shoulders with people at the top of their fields checked another box of my twenty-year plan, and I savored every moment of it—all except for one.

CHAPTER NINETEEN

IT HAPPENED WHEN I was on the subway on my way to work. I had gone to the gym, taken a shower, and headed to the subway station to catch the 6 train to 57th Street, where my office was located. Walking through Madison Square Park, I marveled at the cloudless blue sky and the crisp air. This is why fall is such a popular time to visit New York City. Everything feels clean and vibrant and full of possibility. I exited the elevator and walked into my office to find everyone staring at a television in eerie silence. A plane had just crashed into the North Tower of the World Trade Center. A few moments later, the second plane hit. Time seemed to stop and turn in on itself. Everyone was frozen in shock. Then, the phones started ringing—including mine.

"I can't reach my mom," a panicked Lisa said. Her mom had moved into a condo in Battery Park City, which was a short distance from the Towers. Soon, no one could get through to anyone. The phone lines were jammed, and the cell towers were overloaded as everyone frantically tried to reach their loved ones. Finally, we got through to her mom, who was safe.

We closed the office early, and I joined the throngs of people walking silently and numbly through the streets, making their way back home. I reached Stephanie, who still lived in my building at the time and was headed home, as well. That evening, we were forced to evacuate because of bomb threats to nearby buildings. Stephanie and I walked down to Washington Square Park, not knowing what else to do. Bars remained open and people filled them, sitting in silence, drinking. The silence lingered, as did the smell of the smoldering aftermath.

It took days to understand what had happened. It took longer to process it. Whatever my thoughts were of Islam, this hadn't helped, and the world seemed to feel the same way. I had begun distancing myself from my Pakistani roots and earlier life, and now, if someone asked what my heritage was, I'd say Indian. Hate crimes were on the rise, and Muslims were equated with terrorists.

"This is why you should speak Urdu," said my mother. She was convinced her phone line was tapped by the government.

"We're not talking about anything bad," I countered. "Besides, don't you think they have translators?"

I was annoyed at her ignorance and paranoia. She believed anything anyone told her and refused to think for herself. Meanwhile, my father was devastated. He was a proud American, and now these acts of terrorism tarnished the community he had worked so hard to build. But instead of indulging in fear and paranoia, he encouraged a dialogue between the FBI and his community, which he saw as his duty as a loyal American and a faithful Muslim.

Sometimes people asked me if I felt a backlash of racism after 9/11, but I never did. I lived in one of the most ethnically diverse cities in the world and I didn't look like your typical Muslim. Growing up, I was always mistaken for Greek, Italian, or Spanish, and as an adult, when I traveled to those countries, they took me as one of their own. The only time I felt a racist threat as an adult was in 2022 in Grass Valley, California.

I had stopped at a local doughnut shop and the only people there were a group of white men and the two young blond girls behind the counter. I felt uncomfortable the minute I walked in as their conversation stopped and their stares landed on me. It didn't help that I knew that plenty of people carried guns there. An older white man walked up to me and said, "You got to stay out of the sun. You don't want to get any darker than you already are." I was shaken by his comment and grabbed my order and left. Even though Grass Valley and Staten Island are three thousand miles apart, it seemed that, in some ways, they were closer than I could have expected.

As things slowly returned to the new normal post-9/11, I dove into work again. The next account Paul and I were going to pitch was a huge deal. We were scheduled to go to Pennsylvania for the pitch, but Paul missed the train. I knew what I wanted to say, so I pitched it myself and landed the highly prized and lucrative account. This wasn't the only thing I was to gain.

PART THREE

On Love & Loss

CHAPTER TWENTY

"DOES HE PLAY ON your team or mine?" asked my client, who was gay.

"Mine," I said with a smile.

We were talking about Doug, who had joined a client meeting, was very handsome, and, lucky for me, played on my team—meaning he was straight. I felt an immediate attraction to this gorgeous, green-eyed man with dimples, something I hadn't felt before, and I could tell he felt something too. I also knew that he was also going to be my client.

"We should get together soon so I can update you on the account," I said. We agreed to meet at Bryant Park Grill, which was convenient for both of us.

"Is this a date?" he asked, as our meeting turned from drinks into dinner.

"Do you want it to be a date?" I asked.

The "meeting" ended eight days later. We had quickly become a couple, spending every evening together. This was a new experience for me, and I was reveling in it. I finally met someone that I connected with.

"You know we can't keep working together," I said, keenly aware of the conflict of interest.

A week later, I went into Paul's office and told him to put me on another account. Paul gave me a look. I had to tell him and then swore him to secrecy. It's a good thing we were friends.

In the meantime, life was feeling pretty good. Work was going well, the boundaries (and the Xanax) with my mother seemed to be working a little, which helped diminish the anxiety, and I heard that my dad was passing out my business cards whenever he had the chance. He was proud that I was a senior VP and, even though he didn't understand the intricacies of my work, he knew I was working with some of the world's best companies. It felt like a new chapter in my life had begun. I was breaking through the chrysalis of my past. The metamorphosis was happening, but regardless of my success, my mother refused to acknowledge it. Instead, she did whatever she could to diminish it whenever she had the chance.

One evening, she was having a dinner party, and, partially to please her, I made an appearance. Her friends were happy to see me.

"How are you?" they asked excitedly. "You must be so busy. We haven't seen you in so long!"

Instead of being happy, my mother smirked and crossed her arms.

"I don't know why she works so hard," she said with evident smugness and reproach. "She thinks she's a man, but she'll never be as good as a man." And then she laughed as if to convey how silly I was.

The blood drained from my face. One moment, I felt like I was living my best life and, the next, I was reduced to nothingness. This is the power my mother had over me. Regardless of my accomplishments, it would never be enough. Sometimes, she would ask me how much money I made.

"That's not really your concern," I would tell her.

"But you're my daughter," she'd reply, shocked.

But I knew she wasn't asking for the right reasons. She was asking so that she could tell her friends and brag about it and use the information to build herself up. It was always about her. Boundaries weren't going to change that.

~

I may have been powerless over my mother, but I certainly wasn't powerless over my life plan. I had been at the agency for about two years, which was as long as I was interested in. I was ready to make my move. As if the universe and I were in sync, I received calls from two recruiters within a half hour of each other.

"A major pharmaceutical company is starting a new product communications group," one recruiter said. "Are you interested?"

This was one of the top companies I had dreamed of working with back in my Staten Island hospital days, but it came with a fifty thousand dollar pay cut.

I decided to look at it as a strategic move into the corporate world and trusted that I would make up for it in the future. I didn't know exactly how that would happen, but it was worth the risk. However, I wanted to work on products that could be the difference between life and death for a patient.

At the time, one of the hot new drugs on the market was Viagra, which treats erectile dysfunction. The FDA approved it in 1998, and this company owned the patent. Though I knew I could do great things for that product from a communications standpoint, it wasn't where my interests were. Many people make concessions just to get their foot in the door and then waste valuable time doing things they don't care about. I didn't want to do that. I would compromise on my salary, but not on the types of products I was working on. I made my views clear to them; I still got the job.

The first medicine I was given to work on was the world's best-selling cholesterol drug. It made over nine billion dollars my first year and increased to its peak of thirteen billion by the time I left. Additionally, I was also given the entire cardiovascular portfolio, which totaled over sixteen billion dollars and was the company's priority portfolio. It was a huge responsibility, and I was ready for it.

The first thing I noticed was that an agency had billed the company at least a million dollars for work on a product, but I couldn't find any concrete business returns for that investment. Since I had worked at agencies, I knew how they thought, and because of my business experience in L.A., I kept digging and quickly noticed more of the same. After meeting with the portfolio's leadership team, I came up with a plan. We were going to take a new approach, not just for the company, but for the entire industry. Instead of having parts of our portfolio represented by a bunch of different agencies that were all owned by only three holding companies, we would invite the holding companies to pitch us on the entire sixteen-billion-dollar portfolio. That got their attention.

"This has never been done before. Sounds like a lot of work," the company's corporate leadership said. "Who's going to manage it?"

"I will," I said. Even though it was my idea, everyone would have skin in the game. I would orchestrate it, but it would be everyone's success. Finally, they agreed.

The holding companies created teams from the best people in their agencies and pitched us for the account. It sent ripples throughout the industry and ended up on the front page of the PR trade magazines. I was looked at as a game changer. It was exhilarating particularly because my mother never wanted me to rock the boat even if what people were doing was outdated or wrong. "It's not the way we do things," she'd say. I was supposed to accept the status quo as she saw it, but that was the last thing I wanted to do. I was more interested in blowing up the things that didn't work and smashing through the myopic barriers that stood in the way of delivering more equitable outcomes.

The only downside was that it hastened the demise of my friendship with Paul, which had already started to rupture when we were working together. He was upset that his agency couldn't be part of the bid since I had worked there and it would create a conflict of interest. It wasn't an easy decision to make, but it was the right one and Paul refused to accept it.

I will always go the extra mile for my relationships, but the one thing I won't do is compromise my integrity—especially when I have worked so hard to build it.

CHAPTER TWENTY-ONE

MY RELATIONSHIP WITH DOUG was the icing on the cake of my life. We grew close quickly, but, in any relationship, there are always surprises, and this one came early on.

"I don't want to get married," Doug said. "And I don't want to have kids."

"Okay," I responded.

I wanted both of those things, but I also knew that dating him felt different than anything I had experienced before, and I suspected the same might be true for him. I decided to bide my time. His apartment in Jersey City was being renovated, so he started staying with me. When the renovations finished, he asked me to live with him. We had been dating for about a year.

I decided to sublet my apartment in Manhattan and move in with him and, quickly, we nested. Next came Lola. She was a pug puppy and practically fit into the palm of my hand. Doug and I picked her out, and she was my first pet. I fell in love with her and called her my baby girl. I may not have been ready to tell my parents about Doug, but I was definitely ready for them to meet Lola.

"Why'd you get a dog?" my dad asked with annoyance. From his cultural standpoint, dogs were dirty.

"She's cute," I said. "You'll see."

Lola was now four months old, and, since she had all her shots, I wanted to show her off.

"I'm bringing her over to meet you," I told them.

"Okay," sighed my dad. Up to that point, there had never been an animal inside our family home.

When my dad opened the door, Lola quickly ran inside, past him, and up the stairs to the fourth floor. She was like a tiny heat-seeking missile, and her target was my mother. I chased after her, looking through all the bedrooms until I finally found her in the doorway of my parents' bathroom, wiggling her little tail, and staring at my mother with excitement.

"Allah, Allah!" my mother whispered loudly. She was frozen at the sight of my new puppy, who was less than ten pounds.

"I'm so sorry!" I exclaimed and quickly picked her up. Lola remained absolutely fascinated by my mother. We went downstairs and wherever my mother went, Lola followed.

"She likes you," I told my mother.

My mother looked at the dog as if she was going to attack her.

"She's not going to do anything," I said. "You can pet her."

Over time, my parents got used to her. If I visited the house with her and left the room, I'd come back to find her on the sofa, with my dad, sitting on his chest.

I'd apologize and rush over to pick her up.

"It's okay," he said, petting her. "She is cute."

I even overheard my mother call her darling.

Things were getting serious with Doug, but telling them about him would have to wait. We were already living together, and soon we would buy a weekend lake house together in the Poconos, located in Northeastern Pennsylvania, a short drive from the city. Beautifully situated on Lake Ariel, the location would prove significant in more ways than one.

No one at work knew about my relationship with Doug. First of all, I'm a private person, and, secondly, Doug was working at a company that we were co-promoting a product with. But, before long, paranoia within the company grew and rumors spread.

"The team is incredibly worried that something is going on," my colleague told me. "Doug is dating someone here, and the company is worried that information is being leaked."

It was time to nip the rumors in the bud.

"I'm dating him," I finally admitted. "We've been dating for a few years now. I don't work on that product, and I know nothing about it."

Once people knew that it was me, nobody cared and the mystery was over. A short while later, when I attended a sales award trip in Mexico for my performance, Doug came with me. People knew me and trusted me, and that's what counted.

CHAPTER TWENTY-TWO

"IS YOUR BIGGEST WORRY breast cancer? Think again," read the headline.

I picked up the new issue of *Time* magazine, and on the cover was a silhouette of a woman with a bright red heart. The headline grabbed my attention:

"One out of three women will die of heart disease. What will you do to protect yourself?"

I quickly picked up the phone and called our contact at the American Heart Association. "We have an obligation to do something about women and heart disease," I told him.

"We were thinking the same thing," he replied.

The following week, they were in my office presenting the same pitch deck that they always pitched.

"No," I said. "We need to do something different. I'll build it with you."

I was tapping into the zeitgeist. Around the same time, First Lady Laura Bush kicked off the 2003 Red Dress Campaign to raise awareness of the risk of heart disease in women, and the award-winning book *Women Are Not Small Men* by

Dr. Nieca Goldberg was published, which described the differences in heart disease in women versus men. We needed to be a part of this movement.

In 2000, only 34 percent of women surveyed knew that heart disease was the leading cause of death in women. Like me, most women (and many doctors) thought the leading cause was cancer. Because of that, heart disease was going undetected and untreated. Yet more women than men were dying of it every year. To elevate the issue nationally, I wanted to use science, create guidelines, and involve physicians. I worked with the AHA on the presentation, and, when we were ready, my head marketers and I pitched our plan to the VP of our company. We were given the green light.

Go Red for Women would be the longest and largest sponsorship that my company had done up to that point, lasting three years, and costing six million dollars. It involved the first evidence-based guidelines for women that weren't just drawn from studies done on men.

"You need to talk to the doctors about the issue," our salespeople were told.

In those days, doctor's offices were full of drug representatives from competing companies who were desperately vying for time with physicians to discuss their products. Since our reps were focused solely on the issue of heart disease in women and were the only ones passing out the new guidelines, they got in the door while the other company representatives were not invited in. I felt gratified because we were making a real difference in women's lives. It brought me back to my volunteer days with the woman in the dementia ward whom I couldn't help but who had inspired me to find a way where I could.

It felt additionally gratifying to prove that doing good made good business sense. I tied every idea and strategy to business analytics and proven value. Because I had been told throughout my childhood to believe so many things without questioning them, I had a natural aversion to accepting anything at face value. Therefore, I never accepted the status quo. In this case, I knew the impact my work could have on the business results, and I set about to prove it through ways not typically used in communications.

My work was being discussed in the investor calls and, after I orchestrated a successful data announcement, resulted in moving the company's share price by one point, which is unheard of. This proved something I had long believed to be true: The business of communications, when backed by business strategy, is much more than just "PR." There is inherent business value in it, and it should be prioritized. Growing up in a house of silence hadn't stifled my voice. Instead, I would use it to do good and empower others to do the same.

One of the perks of success is being treated equally by people at the top of their game. Within the company, as it is in many places, there was a bit of the "kiss the ring" culture. Executives, like the president, VP, and CEO sat on a floor far removed from the regular staff. During the holidays, everyone would go to the executive wing of the top floor and shake their hands. I knew the VP from seeing people going to him for approval, and most people were a little afraid of him—he reported to the company's president, after all.

Because of the success of our Go Red for Women Campaign, I was invited to accompany the VP to the ringing of the bell at the New York Stock Exchange. I soon found myself in a car alone with him. As luck would have it, he knew Doug, as they had previously worked together. When I mentioned him, the VP's demeanor completely changed. He opened up and there was an instant rapport. From that point on, whenever our paths crossed at work, he'd always be warm and friendly and ask how I was doing.

"How come he's talking to you?" people would ask in amazement and suspicion.

Since they found him so intimidating, they didn't understand why I was so comfortable with him and why he was so friendly to me. It affirmed for me the truth that no matter who you are or what your position is, people are just people. I was also aware that even at the top, it can get lonely, especially as one's peer group gets smaller and smaller. I think he appreciated the opportunity to connect, which is something, given my childhood, I could understand.

CHAPTER TWENTY-THREE

BY NOW, DOUG AND I had been living together for three years. We had gotten our second dog, Frodo, to keep Lola company since we were traveling a lot. We had our vacation home in Lake Ariel, but we still hadn't had a conversation about getting married. I started cutting out pictures of engagement rings from Tiffany's diamond buying guide and would leave them around the apartment. I know he saw them, but he never said anything, and I never did. I would just casually leave them about. Yet Doug and I would talk about the future and were making life decisions together, so it was time to tell my parents about him.

"I have something to tell you," I started. "I've met someone special."

At this point, I was in my mid-thirties, and I think they were beginning to think anyone would be better than no one, but that didn't stop my mother from spewing a slew of questions at me.

"What kind of background is he from?" she asked. "Is he

Black? Is he Jewish? What do his parents do? When can we meet him? When are you going to get married?"

"I don't know if we're going to get married," I told them. "Or when." But certainly, the expectation was there. Why wouldn't we?

The plan was that we would meet for lunch at an Indian restaurant in the city called Tamarind. Doug was more nervous than I was because, at this point, I was tired of worrying. Enough was enough.

"My dad doesn't speak very much," I warned him.

It turned out as good as could be expected, and I was relieved that the hiding was over. They finally knew about Doug.

The following Christmas Eve, Doug and I were up at our house in the Poconos. We went for a walk in the snow with Lola and Frodo as we usually did, taking the trail through our property past the brook and trees to a large rock that sits at the edge of our property. The rock was covered in snow, on top of which was a bottle of champagne and two glasses.

"What a nice idea for Christmas Eve," I said, turning to Doug to kiss him.

He kissed me softly and said, "You know I love you more than anything. You're the only one in the world to me." Then, he dropped down to one knee.

"Oh my god," I whispered.

Will you marry me?" he asked.

I couldn't have been happier. Even our dogs seemed happy. It was the most romantic moment of my life.

We ran back to the house so I could call my girlfriends. Then we told Doug's mom, who had always been welcoming and warm to me. Then it was time to tell my parents.

My mother was spending the month in India, visiting her brother who was sick, so we decided to tell my father in person and then call my mother afterward. We made plans to take my father to dinner as soon as we got back into town. When we arrived, I could barely wait.

"Dad, I have something to tell you," I said, showing him the engagement ring that I was wearing. "Doug proposed."

"Congratulations," he said, smiling. He was truly happy for me. My mother would be another story.

The next day, I called her and told her. I shouldn't have been surprised.

"Let's not say anything about it now," she said, lowering her voice. "I don't want to tell anyone here."

"Why not?" I asked. She was with her family, after all.

"I want to tell them in my own way," she explained.

I don't know why I was surprised. This seemed like the perfect time to tell her family that her daughter was getting married. Yet, her first response was to keep it a secret.

"Don't tell anyone else in the family," she continued.

"Why not?" I asked, exasperated.

"I don't want them to know it happened when I wasn't there," she explained. Again, it was all about her.

"Fine, but I'm not going to change the date that he proposed," I said.

"No, don't tell anyone!" She persisted. "And, if they ask, I'll come up with another date."

I was incredulous. "Absolutely not," I said. "I refuse to lie."

There was not one ounce of happiness in her voice. I was furious—once again.

CHAPTER TWENTY-FOUR

OUR PLAN WAS TO get married the following November, but, of course, that changed when my mother came back from India.

"Why November?" she asked. "That's too soon, and it'll be too cold."

"We've already waited so long," I explained.

"I'd like my family to come," said my father. He was now the patriarch of his large family, so they would all come out of respect.

"What about next May?" my mother suggested. "It'll give people time to make travel plans."

Out of deference to my father, we agreed to the change.

In the meantime, Doug had changed jobs and was now commuting from Jersey City to Pennsylvania, which is a four-hour drive in each direction, and it was beginning to take a toll on him. We needed to find a new home closer to his work, and, after a brief search, we bought a beautiful home on four and a half acres in Bucks County, Pennsylvania.

Since my work was in NYC, I would need to find a job

closer to our new home, so I reached out to a contact at another large pharma company headquartered in New Jersey. I quickly received a job offer. I couldn't have been more thrilled. Working at the two top global pharmaceutical companies had been part of my twenty-year plan. My dreams were all coming true.

Soon it was time for the wedding planning to begin. My vision was something small and intimate, but Pakistani and Indian weddings are anything but small and intimate, so, of course, my mother had other ideas.

"Who are these people?" I asked, looking at my mother's guest list of over five hundred people. I knew I would have to set some boundaries quickly.

As tradition dictates, my father would pay for the wedding, but just like in college, I wanted to pay for everything else. It would help me in the boundaries department, which came in handy when my mother wanted things like Doug arriving on a white horse. There also are three separate ceremonies in a Muslim wedding. The first day is the ladies' ceremony when the bride-to-be has her hands painted with henna. The second day is the actual wedding, called a Nikah, where the imam usually reads verses from the Qur'an and the couple, along with two male witnesses, sign the Muslim marriage contract. The third day is the reception, which is held by the groom's family.

"Here's what we're doing," I said. "We're only going to have one ceremony. The guest list is capped at two hundred and fifty, and I'm going to choose my own dress."

Traditionally, Indian brides wear gowns made up of bright reds, oranges, turquoise and yellows—and a lot of makeup. This was not my style. I don't like to be the center of attention and tend to wear more subtle colors. I went to the Indian wedding boutique in New Jersey that my mother recommended and found a dress that was cream and gold with a beaded skirt that must have weighed twenty pounds. The dress had long sleeves so that the bride's arms would be covered for modesty, but I arranged to have them removed since the wedding was in May and I could wear a shawl instead.

"I want to see the dress," my mother said. I couldn't say no, so we made a plan to visit the store together. My mother knew the owner socially, and, after we arrived, the very first thing my mother did was apologize for the capri pants and sleeveless blouse that I was wearing. She didn't think it was appropriate to dress so casually in front of people in her community. I couldn't believe she was apologizing for me. It didn't matter that I was a woman in her mid-thirties. I was furious.

"She's dressed fine," responded the owner, who was wearing essentially the same outfit.

When my mother found out I was going to have the sleeves removed from the dress, it was her turn to be furious.

"You can't show your arms!" she cried. "You're going to bring disgrace to our family."

The next hurdle was the wedding ceremony. I didn't want a religious ceremony, but since I knew how much it meant to my parents, I arranged a few meetings with imams, but they didn't go well. I was essentially told that they would only do it if I was a good Muslim. They were afraid their souls would burn in hell "if I didn't take it seriously."

The other issue was that Doug was not Muslim. Women are forbidden from marrying non-Muslim men (whereas Muslim men can marry a Christian or Jew because their children would take the man's religion.)

"Is Doug going to convert?" my parents asked.

"No," I said. "That's a ridiculous question."

I had a cousin whose husband had converted and, from then on, was referred to by his Islamic name. I couldn't imagine calling Doug by any other name.

"Why don't we just elope?" I suggested to Doug. "It'll be less pressure."

Doug looked at me. "You can't do that to your dad," he said, and he was right. I couldn't and neither could he. He really liked my dad, and my dad was very fond of him. "I'll convert," Doug said.

I begged him to change his mind.

"It's not that important to me," he said. "And it will mean so much to your dad."

"Okay," I agreed. However, I would have some stipulations.

"He wants to do it," I told my parents. "But he's not changing his name, and he's not going to suddenly start practicing Islam." I wanted to be clear that there wasn't going to be a sudden religious conversion happening. To me, it was just a technicality.

When the time came, we all went to an uncle's house so he could read Doug the Testament of Faith, known as the Shahada, which Doug then repeated. This was the same uncle who had assaulted me when I was thirteen, but all my rage had been channeled at my mother for not believing or protecting me. I didn't feel anything toward this man except a total lack of respect. I tolerated him because he was dear to my father and had seen him at family functions many times over the years. Of course, I'd never be caught alone in a room with him again. The fact that he was doing this ceremony given the nature of his character epitomized the hypocrisy of many religions, and Islam in particular. My mother cried and made a big deal about it, but to me it was laughable.

Our next task was finding someone to officiate the wedding. I had given up on finding an imam and, instead, found a professor of Islamic studies at Stony Brook University, who, as an Islamic scholar, could help me with the ceremony. The first thing we did was translate the ceremony so that it could be given in both English and Arabic since our guests weren't all going to be Muslim. I also wanted to change what was said at the ceremony.

Regardles of the culture, marriage is a contract and has been seen, in the eyes of the law and religion, as an exchange of property—with the bride being the property. Many traditional marriage vows, regardless of religion, require the bride to submit and obey her husband. Islam is no different. In Islamic marriage ceremonies, the bride often comes in with her eyes lowered and sits on the dais as the male imam or cleric oversees this exchange of property. I had no interest in doing that. As we went over the text, I took out any references to submission, obedience, and anything alluding to a misogynistic and patriarchal exchange of property.

"And I'm not going to lower my eyes," I told my dad.

I had agreed to the tradition of having the bride and groom sit in separate chairs facing the audience with my father and his brother sitting behind me, as well as the uncles.

"I know you are changing the ceremony," said my dad. "The only thing I ask is that you and Doug don't kiss."

I acquiesced. Instead, when the moment came, Doug and I reached out to each other and clasped each other's hands. I caught a glimpse of my father behind me. He was smiling.

Friends and family came from all over the world to celebrate our marriage—some people could only come for one day and flew out the next. We had guests from Pakistan, India, Qatar, London, Washington, D.C., and Chicago. Doug and I worked hard to make sure both Islamic and Western cultures and traditions were honored.

During the cocktail reception, we hired a sitar player and served both Indian and Western appetizers. We also wanted to have an open bar for our friends, which Doug and I would pay for.

"Our people don't drink," said my parents. "So, we don't want our guests seated near the bar."

For dinner, we also offered both a Western buffet and an Indian one.

"Our people don't eat Western food," said my parents. "Don't seat them next to the Western buffet."

We also hired a DJ to play a selection of current and traditional music.

"Our people don't dance," said my parents. "Don't seat our guests near the dance floor."

Because of my parents' wishes, our guests were essentially segregated, with one half of the room being "their people," seated away from the bar, the dance floor, and the Western food, and the other half were "our people."

The funny thing was that when the reception started, the first people at the bar were the Indian men. When the buffets opened, my parents' guests ran over to the Western buffet and, paradoxically, our friends ran over to the Indian buffet. When the dance floor opened, the Indian women were the first ones on it, leading a conga line and grabbing Doug to join them—so much for men and women not mixing.

My parents' heads were spinning, but everyone was having a great time—especially "their people."

"This is the best wedding we've ever been to," said my parents' friends. "We love your dress," gushed my mother's friends.

My mother danced for the first time in her life that night. My dad joined her. We even had to extend the reception for an additional hour because no one wanted to leave.

We had succeeded. We wanted to spend time with our friends and family. We wanted them to be exposed to new things, and most of all we wanted them to have a good time.

"Today is the happiest day of my life," said my dad. "Besides the day you were born."

Even though by this point, my dad's disease had progressed to the point where he was frail and would tire easily, nothing could have diminished his pride and joy on that magical night. My mother, of course, took full credit for the planning of the wedding, even though I did all of it, and she would get to brag about it for years.

Because I was still relatively new in my job, we decided to delay our honeymoon until the end of the year. We were thinking of going to India, but the minute I mentioned it to my father, our romantic itinerary became filled with family visits and requests that we also go to Pakistan to visit more friends and family. I wanted to visit as a tourist, so we quickly changed our plans.

"Let's go to Japan," Doug said, since he had lived there before we met. "I'd love for you to see it."

I happily agreed.

CHAPTER TWENTY-FIVE

SETTLING INTO MARRIED LIFE wasn't that very different from our life before since we had already been living together, and we quickly became busy with work. Joining a new company was a huge culture change from the previous one. Even though both are huge, global companies, the first had a culture of innovation and the second felt more than a little risk averse. It was more about maintaining the status quo even if it meant doing mediocre work. It was more about being comfortable, and even though everyone was warm and welcoming, it felt like people were just waiting to collect their pensions.

Metaphorically speaking, it was the corporate version of my mother lying in bed all day, and I couldn't stand it. I wanted to make things happen. During that time, the company had entered into business development deals for the treatment of hospital-based infections, which afflict roughly 10 percent of all hospital patients—with at least one patient out of that number dying. Since we were launching a new product to address this, I wanted to make sure our global partners felt supported. Often when a global company has a huge footprint in the U.S., the corporate office can make decisions that are not sensitive to other cultures. I was used to navigating between two radically different cultures growing up, and I helped my father do this as well. I also knew how ineffective it was to try to impose one's culture on another, since that's what my mother was always trying to do. To prepare for the launch, instead of creating a one-size-fits-all approach, I called the heads of our offices around the world, in every country, and asked them questions about what they needed to succeed.

"How can I help?" I asked. "What are your concerns?"

It quickly became clear that the challenge was partially in understanding the science behind the treatment, as well as the language and pronunciation of the pathogens involved.

After many conversations and a great deal of thought, I created a package, similar to the Rosetta Stone language program, that contained an audio phonetic glossary to help work through different accents, a bibliography of articles, a listing of key physicians, and fact sheets with images and videos that could be helpful to their teams. The response was unanimously positive. Managers from around the world reached out to express their gratitude because their needs were heard and, because of that, they were able to succeed. This was especially meaningful because of my history of not being heard and not being supported. I also didn't know then how personally affected I'd be by this work until my dad was in the hospital.

~

In most companies, the product that makes the most money is the one that gets all the attention—especially when it comes to stock analysts and investors. We had some blockbuster medicines that yielded enormous returns, but even though the global anti-infectives program wasn't one of them, it would have a huge impact on public health (which we saw when Covid hit in 2020). This was a story I wanted to tell. I wanted investors to see how important this work was. Fortunately, because of how involved I was in the work, the investor relations team came to me to help them shape the narrative so we could make an impact not just in the U.S. but globally. I was focused on business metrics and the dollars-and-cents impacts of the work we were doing that had nothing to do with the number of press releases or arbitrary media impressions. I was, in fact, becoming a global leader helping shape positive healthcare outcomes worldwide. My work was being appreciated, so I thought I would continue to advance within the company. I thought wrong.

I had been told early on that I was on track for a VP role, but it wasn't long before I noticed that a lot of men were getting those promotions, men who knew each other, went to the same Ivy League college, or had the same backgrounds. It felt like the system was rigged and, if I wasn't careful, I would end up being just another cog in the wheel. I wasn't cut out to be a cog. I was willing to give them some time, but not too much time.

I also wasn't cut out for being yelled at again, but I had a strategy for that, and when the time came, I used it. I was on the phone with the CEO and CFO of one of our partner companies and, as they talked, they got angrier and angrier until I was basically being yelled at by two men from Switzerland.

"I can hear that you are really upset," I said calmly. "And I really want to resolve this, so let's take a few minutes to pause, and then why don't you call me back and we can have a constructive conversation."

I quietly hung up the phone. My heart was racing. Had I done the right thing? A few moments later, my phone rang.

"I'm really sorry," said the CEO. "That wasn't fair of us. Let's proceed."

This approach doesn't work when a boss is yelling at you. After working successfully with a couple heads of my department, there had been a reshuffling, and now I was reporting to a woman who could be very harsh. It wasn't long before that harshness was directed at me. This would be my second female boss who seemed more interested in tearing me down than building me up. Someone I had worked for had produced something, and I hadn't given it the attention I should have because I was operating under a false assumption. However, my boss didn't care.

"It's your fault," she yelled. "I blame you!"

I flashed back to my first job at the agency when my female boss would berate me to the point of bullying. It was happening all over again, and I would come home from work full of anxiety. I tried to put myself in her shoes and appreciate the pressure she was under, but, at the end of the day, it was simply demoralizing. We were supposed to be on the same team, but her behavior did nothing to support that.

I had a strategy for that too. I had been compartmentalizing things since I was a child, so I used the same coping mechanism here. Instead of hiding out in my room like I did when I was little, I joined a gym that was on the way to work, which helped me maintain my energy and resilience (and lose the extra pounds I gained moving to the 'burbs). My commute was an hour each way, so, every morning, I would work out with a trainer or take a class, then shower and drive to work.

After work, I'd decompress by calling my dad or a friend, or just listening to the radio. On the weekends, Doug and I would go to Home Depot or Lowe's and do work around the house and garden. It was a great distraction from the anxiety at work and a wonderful way to begin building our married life together. I never had a hard time switching gears from work to homelife, and Doug could always make me laugh. Doug was also a great sounding board. Since he worked in the industry as well, he knew the pressures and personalities and was a great support. Even though he wasn't as much of a risk taker as I tended to be at work, when it came down to it, he always had my back. He was the perfect partner for me, and that would only continue to grow—regardless of the challenges that would come.

Then, in early 2008, I found out I was pregnant. It was a dream come true, and even though Doug was ambivalent about having children, we had made sure our house had enough bedrooms and was located in a great school district. I knew deep down that he'd be a great dad.

Eleven weeks later, I miscarried. It was devastating beyond words, but I never stopped working. It's how I coped. In the meantime, Doug and I began our long IVF journey. While I dove into work, I learned that another man was promoted to VP, and I knew it was time for me to leave. I wanted to steer the ship, not be a passenger on it.

Two weeks later, I got a call from a private company that wanted to go public and wanted me to help them. Since not many people in my position get the opportunity to do this, I was thrilled by the possibility—particularly because I was feeling so stifled by the lack of advancement that was being offered to me regardless of the work I was doing. This would allow me to combine both communications and business strategy while also being more of my own boss. Plus, I was done with being yelled at.

When I left, I felt proud about the work I had done and, apart from my boss, warmly toward those I had worked with. I had accomplished most of my twenty-year plan. I had worked at agencies, then at two of the top global pharmaceutical companies. I had a taste of being my own boss and was ready for more. Despite everything my mother had done to change and diminish me, I was succeeding. I was as good (if not better) than any man. Even if I wasn't promoted to VP by the boys' club, my talents and accomplishments were being acknowledged and rewarded—something I never experienced as a child at home. I still struggled with anxiety, but apart from that, I had built a wonderful life, far different from my parents' or the oppressive one my mother wanted for me. My dream of being married had come true, and despite the awful miscarriage, we were working on getting pregnant. On some level, I felt that if I held that vision in my sight clearly enough, it would have to happen. Everything else had.

CHAPTER TWENTY-SIX

THE WEEK I STARTED my next job, my father was rushed to the hospital. I left work immediately. I hadn't even met the CEO yet, so leaving, even for a family emergency, was not a great way to start. But I didn't have a choice. I explained the situation and drove from New Jersey to Staten Island. I had just seen my dad less than a week prior when we celebrated his birthday. He hadn't been feeling well, so, instead of taking him out to dinner, Doug brought some steaks and an iron skillet, and we cooked dinner there. I expressed concern about his health then and begged him to have tests done.

"You have to see your doctor," I told him.

Since he was a double kidney transplant patient, his immune system was compromised, and I was right to be worried. He had developed a *c. difficile* infection—exactly the kind of infection treated by the antibiotics I had worked on at my last job.

When I got to the hospital, they told me what happened. He had been doing his Thursday office hours and started feeling increasingly ill but wouldn't stop working. Finally, his staff drove him to the same hospital where he used to be an attending physician. People knew him there. That comforted me. It was August 25. A month later, they would transfer him to another hospital, where he would stay until the end of October.

During those months, I would work during the day, make the hour and a half drive to visit him in his hospital room, and then drive home late at night. I was so exhausted one night that when I pulled into the garage, I hit the side of the wall. I wasn't only stressed about my father; I was stressed about having to manage my mother. I needed to take care of them both. It was too much. And then, I realized he wasn't going to come home—ever.

I walked inside and my mother said, "I washed and ironed all of his clothes so they will be ready when he comes home."

She either didn't know about the severity of my father's condition or was in denial. I felt truly sad for her. She had gone from living in her father's house in India, where she had been completely taken care of, to marrying my father and being taken care of by him for almost forty-one years. What would she do without him?

Once again, I had to compartmentalize. I was aware of what my mother needed, yet I also needed to focus on my father's care—especially when the residents and attending physicians seemed to be dismissive. I knew I had to take matters into my own hands, as I had so often in my life. Since I knew how hospitals worked, I wrote a letter to the hospital CEO knowing that everyone would read it, which would make him accountable. I described the lack of attention and care for my father and how he had been a member of the hospital and community for over forty years, training some of their very own physicians. That got their attention.

Practically overnight, the dynamic changed. Suddenly, I had meetings with doctors, nurses, and specialists—essentially everyone on the care team. There was not a minute when I didn't know what was happening. The letter also got the word out to the rest of the medical community, which was helpful since many of the doctors who were trained by my father hadn't even known that he had been admitted. Doctors and nurses came up to me and told me how my father had touched their lives.

Ultimately, it didn't help, other than getting him the care he needed and making sure that he was comfortable. Soon, he was transferred to the ICU. I knew my father didn't want to die in the hospital and preferred, instead, to be in the comfort of his home. When one of his partners wanted to continue administering dialysis, I stopped her.

"We have to do it," she insisted.

"But it's not helping," I countered.

The only thing that seemed to help him was when he saw familiar faces. When the longtime staff from his office came in, "his girls" as he called them, his face would light up and his spirit came alive. I begged him to hang on.

"I want you to meet your grandchild," I cried.

He knew about my miscarriage and that I was still trying to conceive.

"I want you to live your life now," he said. "You've done enough to take care of this family."

Soon, he stopped talking except to occasionally ask what day it was through his fog.

Doug came to visit him and held his hand. "I'm going to take care of her," he said. "Don't you worry."

I begged him to hold on. He didn't know about the IVF or my subsequent miscarriages, but I wanted him to meet his future grandchild. I would spend the night in the chair next to his bed, terrified to leave. Lisa came to be with him, as well as other close friends and family members who offered their blessings.

The next morning, I drove home to get my things and went upstairs and screamed. I just lost it. It was all too much. There was nothing I could do to keep him alive. I couldn't compartmentalize the pain away. Crying, I packed all my black clothes, knowing that I wouldn't be home until after the funeral. I called hospice, then drove back to the ICU and brought him home.

"What day is it?" my dad whispered the next morning. We had music playing softly in the background and someone had come to read the Qur'an.

"Dad, It's Jumu'ah," I said, softly. *Jumu'ah* means Friday in Arabic. "It's okay to go now."

A few minutes later, he took his last breath. I found out later that every Friday for over fifty years, my father had left his office to do his Friday prayers at the mosque. It felt like no mistake that this was the day he passed.

Hospice called the funeral home while my mother called her family and the imam to let them know. I lay with him until they took him away. My mother was crying in the background.

"God should have taken me," she wailed.

As awful as it sounds, I remember thinking, "He took the wrong parent."

Soon the doorbell started ringing. In the Islamic community, word spreads quickly, and people just show up at the house, invited or not. Though they came to pray, it felt intrusive. I just wanted a moment to myself. I dragged myself to the bathroom and brushed my teeth. I wasn't wearing any makeup, and I had barely slept. My mother flashed me an angry and disapproving look. She didn't like the fitted black V-neck sweater I was wearing.

"This is not the time," I said to her sharply. Even on the saddest day of my life, she couldn't stop criticizing me.

When I called the newspaper with the obituary I had written for him, they told me they were devoting a full page to him.

"We've known your father since he first came to Staten Island," they said. "He's done so much for our community. He deserves more than a standard obituary."

Since my father touched the lives of many within Staten Island, we decided to go ahead with a public viewing even though it's not typically done in Islamic tradition. The line of people who came to honor him went out the door. I was grateful for my friends that could come. Lisa and her mom were by my side, as well as my friends Mary and Andrea and, of course, Doug.

After the viewing, we went to the mosque that my father had helped found in order to do prayers. As is tradition, the men were downstairs with my father's body while the women were segregated on a balcony above. It didn't matter if I was his daughter, that's where I was supposed to be. I looked down at the men and fumed.

When we arrived at the cemetery for the burial, over a hundred people were already there, and, like at the mosque, the men were in the front and the women were behind them. I pushed my way to the front. I wasn't about to let them keep me away from my father.

Unbelievably, when I started to cry, I was admonished to stop.

"Be strong," the men told me.

While I was touched by their outpouring of support, I was also furious at their patriarchal and misogynist attitudes. Though these archaic attitudes also exist in the business world, in the Muslim community they felt more pronounced. Perhaps what was worse, the women accepted it and submitted to it, and then passed it onto the next generation of girls. That's what my mother tried to do. Today, many Middle Eastern women are speaking up at great risk to themselves, and some men support them. But, back then, I felt alone, betrayed, and outraged.

CHAPTER TWENTY-SEVEN

"WHY DON'T YOU MOVE back home with your mother for a while?" asked an aunt. I wished she were joking, but I knew better.

"I'm married and live in Pennsylvania and work in New Jersey," I said. "I don't think that's going to work."

"But what about your mother?" she pleaded.

"I guess we'll have to figure it out," I answered.

My biggest fear had come true. My mother was alone, and everyone was looking to me to take care of her. Caretaking often falls on the women in families (and elsewhere), and though I may have been the son my father never had, I was very much expected to fulfill the daughter role, as well.

I might have felt differently if my mother hadn't been coddled her whole life, or if she had treated me with care instead of emotional abuse, or if every therapist hadn't told me all the ways that I was supposed to change to accommodate her insanity instead of safeguarding mine. I might have felt differently—but I didn't. Yet every weekend after my father passed, I visited her. I made sure she had food and that she was safe. I took care of the finances, the insurance, and everything else.

During all of this, I was still trying to have a baby. It wasn't lost on me that I was turning forty. The doctors in Pennsylvania had done a number of tests and found several fibroids. I had endometriosis in my mid-thirties when Doug and I were first dating and had multiple D&Cs, which resulted in scar tissue that also needed to be removed. After that, I did IVF numerous times and had several miscarriages. Each loss doesn't get easier. It just gets worse. I tried switching doctors to one in New Jersey and then went to one of the best infertility specialists in Manhattan, who had written numerous books and focused on higher-risk patients.

I was grateful we could afford multiple IVFs, but there's a difference between what you can afford and what your body or marriage can bear. Doug would give me the shots, our sex was becoming a chore, and every time I got pregnant and miscarried, it was like we'd go into our separate corners to grieve. No one talked about these things back then. Today, people post it to their social media. I would think back on my early thirties, before I had met Doug, when I had considered freezing my eggs, which was a new procedure at the time, but I never thought I'd have a problem having a child. My childhood friends and colleagues were on their second child, and though I was happy for them, I was falling into a pit of despair and would cuddle with my dogs and cry.

Lucky for Doug and me, we already had a track record going to therapy. Doug had suggested it when we first got married, not because we were experiencing any issues but because of both of our backgrounds. He had grown up with a father who was far less than ideal, and we used to joke that his father should have married my mother. They were both toxic to us, so we wanted to make sure we weren't bringing that baggage into our marriage. In fact, his father told him not to marry me, while he had been married several times. In other words, he wasn't the kind of person you want to take marriage advice from. On top of that, he never liked me, and I found out later just how much so, but Doug always protected me from that. He always took care of me and prioritized our marriage and relationship, so when the IVF was causing a schism between us, he found us a therapist we could go to for support. I don't think my mother had a paradigm for this kind of male-female relationship. She once asked me about it after Doug and I were first engaged.

"Does he treat you with respect?" she asked. "Does he treat you like a partner?"

I nodded.

"That must be so nice to be treated like a partner," she replied. It was one of the only times I saw a crack in her hard shell.

Throughout the IVF, therapy, and new job, I was doing everything I could to help my mother after my father died. She had fallen down, and I needed to find her a better place to live. I was cleaning out their house and basement to get it ready to sell, and since my mother was a bit of a hoarder, there was a lot to do. Every time I saw her, I would leave with a stomachache from the stress. She seemed incapable of being nice. After she was horrible to me while I was in the process of helping her, I snapped at her.

"I didn't realize you had so little respect for me," she said.

"Respect is earned," I retorted.

During one of the IVF implantations, my doctor

reminded me not to lift anything, which would delay the work I was doing to help my mother move. One afternoon, I had a weak moment and confided in my mother about the IVF and miscarriages.

"It's not my fault you can't have a baby," she responded. "You're old. You waited too long."

Finally, I found an adult community that she liked that also had an assisted living facility attached, just in case she needed it. Regardless of my feelings about my mother, I wanted the transition to go smoothly. She had lived in that home for most of her life, and moving her could be enormously destabilizing. To ease the change, I customized her unit with cabinets and fixtures that matched the ones from the house. I made sure the carpet and paint were similar, as well. At night, I would make the now two-and-a-half-hour drive in each direction to meet with the contractor, buy her new furnishings, and arrange the sale of the house—all while keeping up with the IVF. I wasn't sure how much more I could handle. I would drive home late at night after seeing her and imagine turning the wheel and crashing into a tree. No more pressure, no more anxiety, no more grief. But the thought was only temporary. I had a husband and a life that I cared about. We were trying to build a family, yet I was sacrificing everything for someone who didn't care about me. My mother only cared about what I could do for her. At what point does it stop?

After she moved, she flourished. She made friends with men for the first time in her life and was going to laughter yoga classes, movies, and museums. I was happy for her. Even though I had no real love for her, I could have empathy—the empathy that she could never have for me or anyone else.

Now that she was settled, I needed to take care of myself and focus on work. Doug and I had spent tens of thousands of dollars on fertility treatments, and nothing was working. The stress wasn't helping. Still, she would hound me if I didn't call her or come by.

"Where have you been? You just dumped me here," she'd say. I felt like I was drowning, and she would just keep piling it on.

I finally realized that she didn't care that I was hurting. She only cared about what I could do for her. All she did was take and I just kept giving—and never once did she say thank you. I knew that all this stress and anger was detrimental to my health and that of my future baby. In fact, it felt like it was killing every child I was trying to have. I had tried everything: acupuncture, herbs, retreats, and multiple therapists, but nothing was working. Finally, I found a therapist who specialized in a tapping technique to help regulate overwhelming feelings. Not only was I dealing with the historical baggage with my mother, but I was also grieving the multiple miscarriages and the loss of my father, all while dealing with a demanding new work environment.

"Why is my body failing me?" I'd ask. "Why can't I do this? Having a baby is supposed to be natural."

During the tapping, the therapist gave me phrases to say, such as "I am worthy of love. My body is strong. I am worthy of a child." After some time working together, she finally said to me what no other therapist had suggested.

"Why don't you take a break from her?" she asked.

"I can't do that," was my first reaction.

"She's a very toxic person for you," she said. "She's not suffering the consequences of that. You are. You are the one who isn't sleeping. You are the one with anxiety. You are the one feeling awful."

I nodded.

"So why don't we remove that stress?" she asked.

It wasn't an easy decision to make, but it was either my life or hers. I stopped returning her calls and, suddenly, everything changed. The anxiety I suffered from my whole life immediately disappeared. I didn't have an anxiety problem. I had a mother problem. I got off the Prozac that I had been on throughout my twenties and thirties, and now that I was just over forty, I was finally free of her.

During all of this, I was helping the company prepare for its initial public offering (IPO) to transition from being privately owned to being publicly owned. It was an exciting opportunity. Yet, once again, I compartmentalized my emotions and let my rational brain take over. I would feel the feelings later.

From March to November, I worked with the securities lawyers and bankers on crafting language that would tell a compelling business story, and often I was met with initial resistance.

"We can't do that," they would say.

"Why not?" I'd ask. Besides two female lawyers, I was the only woman in a room full of men.

"Well, I suppose, technically, we could," they would always end up saying.

"Great, then let's do it," I'd say.

Negotiating a business strategy to create dynamic narratives combined everything that I loved: business, science, finance, law, and, of course, communications. When we were done, investors said it was one of the best-written documents they had seen. However, the IPO ended up being withdrawn, which was disappointing, but, during that time, a meaningful opportunity arose. The FDA contacted us because they wanted to obtain an emergency use authorization for our respiratory product in order to combat the SARS virus. The CDC had declared that the SARS virus had the potential to pose a severe threat to public health. We realized that we could offer public health value by working with government affairs. We quickly convened a group of thought leaders that included nurses, physicians, pediatricians, and emergency services experts and outlined areas that needed critical improvement in the event of a global pandemic that could cripple the U.S. hospital infrastructure. This was in 2012.

Another pressing public health issue was end-of-life care, which was close to my heart since I had just confronted it when I insisted on taking my father home to die instead of keeping him in the ICU. Most people prefer to die at home rather than in a hospital, yet millions of dollars in care are wasted in the futile attempt by grieving family members to keep their loved one alive, despite little hope of recovery and despite the patient's expressed wishes. We ended up co-authoring a bipartisan end-of-life bill that passed both houses of Congress. This kind of work was a lifeline during an immensely difficult time personally. It felt enormously gratifying to do something that could impact the lives and safety of millions of people when I couldn't seem to positively impact my own fertility.

The company then decided to separate R&D from the commercial business, and it was time for me to move on. I had been there six years and during that time had gotten pregnant and miscarried a dozen times.

CHAPTER TWENTY-EIGHT

"MAYBE WE SHOULD STOP trying," Doug said. "We could look at adoption."

We were about to leave for California, where we had decided to relocate. The West Coast was attractive for a variety of reasons. The CEOs there seemed more accessible, and the companies were bold and innovative. Plus, with all the losses and Hurricane Sandy on top of it, we were ready to start somewhere new. I was not ready to stop trying to get pregnant, and when I heard those words, I felt like a failure. I felt betrayed by my body. I never got angry at Doug, but after all the stress and grief over the last six years, I just lost it. I couldn't hold my feelings in any longer.

I ran out to the garage and jumped in my car. I had to get away. Fight, flight, and freeze are trauma responses, and I was in full flight. I smashed my phone to the ground so he couldn't call me and peeled out of the driveway into the night. It had been storming, and the rain was still coming down. I drove to an empty park and screamed and cried. I was gone for hours. I just needed to be by myself.

When I finally came home, I found Doug crying because he was so worried.

When we got to California, he signed us up for adoption seminars, and when we had our final visit, the woman told us about all of the horrible situations that could happen, that there were no guarantees, and the mother could change her mind at the last second. I was tired of having my heart broken over and over again. I didn't think I could bear it another time.

"I'll give you a few moments to think about it before you sign the paperwork," she said and left the room.

Doug broke down. "I want to still try to have our biological child."

So, against the odds, we would try again.

When we had decided to move to California, we agreed that whoever got the best offer and relocation package would be the first to go, with the other to soon follow. In no time, I received not one offer but two. Soon, I would be reminded how important it is to trust one's instinct.

~

The first company had invited me to fly out to San Francisco, and I arrived late Thursday night for my interview the following day. In the meantime, another recruiter called me about a different company that was also interested in meeting with me, but, since I was traveling, they were told that I wasn't going to be available for a couple days.

As I exited the airport, my cell rang.

"This is going to sound crazy," the recruiter said. "But the other company still wants to meet with you and they want to do it tonight at their board meeting. Everyone will be there."

"I can't," I said.

I had just flown six hours, hadn't taken a shower, and was famished. Plus, I hadn't had any time to research them and knew virtually nothing about the company.

"Check into the hotel and take a shower," he said. "They're going to send a car for you."

I got out of the shower and, while I dressed, I had the recruiter on speaker so he could walk me through the company and the opportunity. When the car arrived, I jumped in and headed to their headquarters in Sunnydale, where dinner was waiting for me. I met with the board and a few key people and then returned to my hotel.

The next day, I went to the first company where my interview was scheduled and met with Matthew, the founder and CEO. I was instantly impressed. Matthew was personable, charismatic and, most of all, genuine. He was also a big-picture thinker, so there was an instant connection, but, unfortunately, it wasn't the right opportunity for me. I left their offices on Market Street and called Doug, disappointed.

"I would love to work with him someday," I told him.

After I returned home, I wrote Matthew a letter thanking him for the interview and expressed my desire to stay in touch. Then, my phone rang. The recruiter told me that the other company wanted to fly me out to California again and that they probably wanted to make an offer.

I got back on a plane to California, where I met with the CEO. He explained his vision for my role and, again, it missed the mark. I knew I could do more.

When I got home, I emailed him and politely declined, adding that I thought there was more work that the company needed to do. He called me the next day.

"I'd like to talk to you about this," he persisted. "What do you think we should be doing?"

As always, I told him the truth.

He listened and then said that he wanted me to talk to his right-hand person, the chief operating officer. Within days, I received a very lucrative offer and, instead of being a lateral move, it would put me where I wanted to be—in the executive suite as an SVP.

Just to be safe, I reached out to my network to see what others knew about the company and its culture.

"It's a tough environment," I was warned. "You have to have sharp elbows, but that should be easy for you. You're from New York."

Doug and I moved to Santa Clara, California on the Fourth of July weekend of 2014. We still had to sell our house in Pennsylvania, so after Doug helped me get set up and comfortable, he headed back to put the property on the market.

The following Monday after the move was my first day, and I was asked to make a presentation to the board introducing myself and my plans for the future. It felt like a whirlwind, but nothing I wasn't used to. I started building my team, and I was feeling good.

The goal was to increase the company's value, and I was given a target that I was expected to hit. One of the reasons I took the job was because the company had a great product with multiple uses. It was an entire pipeline of products in one pill. I knew I could sell it, and that, with an asset like that, people should and would be clamoring for it. I immediately set to work.

The pill was approved by the FDA, and we partnered with a large pharmaceutical company—one that I had worked at previously. Now it was my turn to be on the small company side instead of with big pharma, and my job was to fight for our interests.

I'm one of the people who always read contracts before I sign. I do the same with business agreements so I can understand where the grey areas are, where the opportunities are, and where we can push back if needed. Right away, I saw issues (and opportunities). The first one was that the clinical site had certain publication rights, and I wanted to change that. I met with the general counsel and advocated for our rights to publish so I could use it to affect the company's positioning in the market. We did just that.

Next, I wanted us to be the "partner of choice" since we were partnering with some of the world's largest pharmaceutical companies. I knew that doing so had the potential to move the stock price.

Professionally, it was an extremely rewarding time, but personally, it was draining. Though I had started in a strong position and had built a great team, things were beginning to turn. I thought I was going through perimenopause because I wasn't sleeping. Later, I realized it was just the prolonged stress of working there. But they didn't know who they were dealing with. I couldn't wait to leave, but I also wasn't going to let them force me out. I had worked too hard to make the company successful.

I quietly bided my time. Within six months, I helped increase the market cap from $8 billion to $19.8 billion, meeting their target and exceeding it.

During this time, Doug and I needed to move out of our temporary apartment before our relocation package expired. I had my eye on Menlo Park with its beautiful tree-lined streets, but, at the time, there was only one house for sale. We put in an offer, and, despite the competition, got it.

Finding a house and moving into it may seem like a lot to do when you're already working around the clock and not sleeping, but, as they say, if you want to get something done, ask a busy person. Doug and I have always juggled multiple things at once, and it's actually easier when you are in a constant state of momentum than trying to motivate yourself from a standstill. Plus, as usual, it was a great distraction from the negativity at work.

The company was soon acquired for $21 billion, which was the second largest acquisition in the industry at the time. I received my payout and left.

I wish that leaving would have been the end of my troubles. Instead, I received veiled threats and heard through my professional network that there were lies being spread about me. It was quite ironic. And after all I had given to this company, it was disappointing.

Within a couple weeks, I emailed Matthew.

"I'm done," I wrote.

A few minutes later he emailed me back.

"I'd love to see you," the email said. We met for lunch, and it was like no time had passed.

"I don't think we were ready before," he said over a plate of shared french fries, but now they were doing a reboot and bringing on new leadership.

"I really want you to work with me," he finished.

I met a few of the other key people within the company and started right away.

The culture couldn't have been more different. Matthew wrote his team one of the nicest introductory emails about me and what I was going to do at the company. I was reminded of why I liked Matthew initially and the trepidation I felt, in comparison, after meeting the company that I ultimately went with. From then on, I would always listen to my gut. Doing so has always benefited me in the past.

Matthew wanted me to help with the company's investor strategy since I had proven my chops before. It was promising. They had a great product on the market and had acquired an oncology drug for metastatic breast cancer. They were also in a co-promotion with a difficult partner, so the first thing I had to do was deal with that—particularly because they had signed off on a number of things that I took issue with.

"I'm not spending two-hundred and fifty thousand for that," I told the partner.

My partner, a young man with an arrogant attitude, wasn't pleased by my response, and it set the tone for our relationship moving forward.

I dove into the details and did some recalibrating. My contact felt threatened, even though my role was higher than his, and he continued to be difficult to work with.

"I don't care if you're vice president!" he'd scream. I'd sigh and hang up the phone. I didn't take his behavior personally. Mostly, I found it amusing.

~

During all this time, Doug and I kept up our efforts to have children. While it was a lot all at once, keeping busy at work meant life was more than having my heart broken each time we suffered another loss. In truth, we were getting tired—the doctor appointments, the invasive procedures, the Chinese herbal teas, the supplements, the acupuncture, the reiki, and the meditations. We were exhausted, and we often retreated to our own corners, ashamed of our individual and collective failures, alone in our inability to comfort each other or stop trying. It was a hard period, but we continued on, against all odds.

And then, it happened. Doug and I became the parents of two beautiful twin daughters, Lily and Elle. Our joy, relief, and transformation was almost too much for words. At long last, our family was complete. It was magic.

Work continued, and I can remember being on a call with that same difficult partner again, with him yelling at me again. Later, it got back to him about the fact that I just had newborns and that people had overheard him yelling at me. He was embarrassed by his behavior.

"I didn't know you were on maternity leave," he scoffed.

"How is it any of your business?" I asked. "You shouldn't be yelling at anyone, regardless of the circumstance." I always kept my personal life private no matter what was going on.

My maternity leave consisted of only a few days because the company had found itself in the middle of a hostile takeover attempt while, at the same time, one of our patents was facing a challenge by the U.S. government with Bernie Sanders signing off on it, a week before his presidential news, which made it front page news.

I flew to Washington on a Sunday to prepare our response in case Matthew found himself testifying before Congress. Doug and I had scheduled a nanny to come help while I was gone, but then the agency called and said that the nanny had taken another job.

"What are we going to do?" Doug asked me. I had just landed at Dulles International Airport. We decided that because I was already in D.C., I would stay for the first set of morning meetings and then fly home the next day.

When I got back, Doug looked like the walking dead. He handed me the babies and then passed out in our bedroom. He had been awake with our two newborns for thirty-six hours straight. Now, after a long flight and working through the weekend, it was my turn.

Five o'clock the next morning, I was on a call with the D.C. lawyers while holding both babies on my chest. To make things a little easier throughout this extremely intense period, I'd spend Wednesday nights at the Palace Hotel by our offices in San Francisco. This eliminated the commute, which was more than an hour each way.

We successfully resisted the hostile takeover, but we weren't out of the woods yet, for it had pushed the company into a bidding war. Fortunately, at the same time, the government's claim against our patent had stalled, so we were only dealing with one emergency.

A few months later, the company was acquired. I had been at the company seven months and helped increase the market capitalization of the company from six billion dollars to thirteen billion. The company sold for $14.3 billion dollars in an all-cash deal—the second high value acquisition I was to be a part of in less than two years.

CHAPTER TWENTY-NINE

NORMALLY, I WOULD BE thinking about what my next career move would be, and I would do that eventually, but first, I had two babies to spend time with. The nature of my work was an all-or-nothing endeavor, and the intensity required hyperfocus, leaving little room for my personal life. The payoff was not only the professional growth and gratification of doing a job well but also the contribution to building my family's wealth and security.

Finally, I could take a few months off to breathe, and my life felt nothing less than idyllic. Doug had a motorcycle, and sometimes we would go for rides through the beautiful Northern California coastal redwoods. I found it so comforting to wrap my arms around his waist, and he would always tease me that he knew I was relaxed when my helmet would hit him because I had fallen asleep.

Our 1,100-square-foot house was close to a neighborhood park, so we'd walk there with the twins and our two dogs almost daily. We settled into a comfortable routine. Friday nights would be wine and cheese nights, and Doug loved picking out the cheeses and setting everything up. He loved cooking, and I was happy to do the dishes. Some evenings, he would sit on our deck and smoke a cigar; I'd play with the twins, or, if they were sleeping, relax on the couch in front of the TV.

It may seem simple and mundane, and it was. This was the perfect life I had always yearned for. I had my handsome, dimpled, green-eyed husband, two beautiful girls who got their Daddy's dimples, and our two dogs. We lived in a beautiful house in a nice neighborhood; the weather was always wonderful, and we didn't have any financial concerns. After a lifetime of feeling like a whole part of me was missing and out of my grasp, I finally identified what it was: safety and security. I felt safe and secure. How could that not be the perfect life?

And Doug was a born father—something I had known from day one. I'm glad I trusted my instincts even when he was saying he didn't want children. He diapered them like a pro. He bought every child-rearing book and read them. I don't think I even gave them a bath for the first eighteen months of their lives. He had it mastered and relished every second of it, saying that his greatest source of fulfillment was being a dad.

I relished that my daughters would have such a close relationship with their daddy early on since my relationship with my father only grew as I entered adulthood. Doug was the kind of dad every little girl wishes for, and though Doug and I may not have been on the same page about getting married when we first met, we were very much on the same page about everything else, including our parenting styles. Both of us knew early on that we were going to put the twins on a sleep schedule. We decided to use the Ferber method; they were soon sleeping through the night, and so were we. When we'd run into other parents, the conversation would invariably go like this:

"Oh, you have twins?" they'd exclaim. "You must be exhausted!"

"No, actually," we'd reply. "They sleep through the night."

Some parents seemed aghast at the thought. "They're sleeping throughout the night?!" they'd say, incredulously. It seemed like their shock was actually more about their disappointment that we couldn't commiserate with them, and, occasionally, there were parental microaggressions that would get to me.

One day, when I was picking up baby formula at our neighborhood Target, a woman walked behind me and snarled, "Breast is best!" I was so angry and taken aback, I had no words. That behavior certainly isn't kind and, worse, it's extremely unsupportive of women and parents, in general. But both of our girls were healthy and happy. We were clearly doing something right.

Perhaps we were reaping the rewards of having children later in life—as unintentional as that had been. We were fully ensconced in our adult lives, and so it seemed to make more sense to have the babies fit into that, instead of upending it to fit into some preconceived or outmoded approach to parenting. A byproduct of this approach was that we were well-rested and well-resourced parents. If we had abandoned everything that made us who we were, we would ultimately be abandoning our children. Since we were at home in our lives with our children, we were better equipped to parent versus being stressed out and short-tempered.

We employed the same philosophy with their diet, as well. Instead of becoming parents who only feed their kids buttered noodles and chicken fingers, our girls would eat everything from lobster to legumes. Instead of making two separate meals, we made one—the family meal.

However, because food allergies are such a growing issue with children, we tested our girls when they were four months old and talked to our doctor to make sure we used the latest guidelines. Fortunately, given our backgrounds working in pharma, we knew how to interpret clinic data, but, as any parent knows, doing everything right doesn't necessarily protect your children, which was something I was hyperattuned to since I felt so unprotected by my own mother. Regardless, I would have to face my own feelings of powerlessness sooner than I would have liked, and it wouldn't be the last time.

It seemed to come out of nowhere. I was on the phone with work when the nanny frantically ran into the room with one of my babies seizing. I hung up the phone mid-conversation and called 911 while holding her tightly.

Being able to power through intense situations without emotion can pay off in moments like this. We rushed to the Lucile Packard Children's Medical Center at Stanford, and I held her as she was poked and prodded by the medical team. It wasn't until we got home, hours later, that I finally broke down in tears. The idea of anything bad happening to my babies terrified me.

It turned out that my daughter had a febrile seizure. She went on to have one more before she was diagnosed with recurrent ear infections that required inserting tubes into her ears. After that surgery, she didn't have any more seizures.

Throughout my life, I had always been told not to show

emotion. In fact, Doug used to say that I was the best person to have around in a crisis, because I'm unflappable. It was loving Doug and having him love me back that broke the hardness in me. I could finally cry at movies and become emotional at emotional times. And while the habit of shutting off my emotions is not good for long-term emotional health, I can always count on thinking clearly without emotions clouding my judgment in times of crisis. And this was one of those times where it came in handy.

CHAPTER THIRTY

AFTER MATTHEW'S COMPANY WAS acquired, he became
the CEO at an East Coast company that was working on
a new late-stage Alzheimer's drug. He wanted me to join
him. I knew I didn't want to go back to New York, but I was
excited by the prospect of working on a drug that could help
so many, especially since there had been little progress in
the treatment of Alzheimer's for over 16 years, when Doug
had coincidentally helped launch Aricept®, the world's first
approved drug for treating Alzheimer's. I thought back to
my early years volunteering on the dementia ward at the
hospital and how it had brought me to the point of tears. I
knew then that I wanted to do something to help. This was
my chance.

Though the company didn't have an approved product
yet, this would be an opportunity to work on their first—if
it worked. It was a huge risk, but I felt it was one worth
taking, so Matthew and I struck a compromise. Instead of
moving back to New York, I would commute, not from
California, but from Austin, Texas, since it was a direct

flight and closer in time zones than California. It was time for us to move again.

Doug and I knew that we liked Austin because, years earlier, he had started going to Formula 1 races around the world. He had a friend who was also into the races, and he saw him so frequently that I would teasingly call him his boyfriend. Finally, I realized that if I was ever going to see my husband, I better get into Formula 1, so I did in 2012 with a trip to the Grand Prix at the Circuit of the Americas track in Austin. It quickly became one of our favorite things to do, and we often would envision living there. The time had come.

Dripping Springs is a rural city only 30 minutes outside of Downtown Austin and made up of "open spaces and friendly faces," most of which are young professionals and their families. Our house was five times the size of our home in Menlo Park, had a pool in the backyard, and was on nearly an acre. My parents may not have given me swim lessons when I was younger, but I wasn't about to make that mistake with my girls. They would grow up knowing how to swim and ride bikes and not be afraid to play outside.

Around this period, the company that Doug was working at was also acquired.

"Why don't I stay home with the girls?" he offered. "Then you can commute and not worry."

He quickly got to know all the moms in our cul-de-sac and would be the one swapping recipes and child-rearing tips with them. Previously, he wouldn't necessarily start a conversation with strangers, but now, with the girls, he would chat up other parents about their kids, especially if they had twins. His mother would come to help, and we also hired nannies and created a healthy support system so our family could flourish. At that point, the twins were young enough that they didn't seem to notice too much when I was gone. Soon enough, that would change.

In the meantime, I became what is called a super commuter, flying out of Austin every Monday morning at 6:15 and returning Thursday evening. On Fridays, I would work from home and then spend time with Doug and the twins on the weekends.

It felt good to be back in New York. The work was intense but rewarding. Our goal was to develop this potential treatment for Alzheimer's, get FDA approval, and then bring it to patients. Mondays, when I arrived in New York, I'd take the train directly to our offices in Times Square. Most nights after work, we'd have working dinners. In the rare free moments, I would grab a drink with my New York girlfriends, see my old hairdresser and doctors, and marvel at the beauty and excitement of the city. Even though it was no longer my home, it had been a hugely meaningful part of my life, and being there felt deeply affirming.

Thursday nights came quickly, and I'd be back on a plane, flying home to see Doug and the girls. Then, before I knew it, Sunday evening would roll around and I'd find myself kissing the girls goodnight, knowing that I wouldn't see them the next morning, or the next. The goal was to make the transition seamless so the girls wouldn't notice since they were so young. I would take on the stress to make it work, and Doug was my rock, as he always had been, supporting me, taking care of the house and the moves and the girls. He was happy to do it, and it made me happy to see him flourish in that way.

One Thursday evening, I caught an earlier flight home and, when I got there, I rushed into the playroom to hug the twins. They held onto me like never before. The time had come. They were beginning to notice when I was away, and they were beginning to miss me. I gulped back the tears. I missed them too, and feeling their little arms clinging to me was almost more than my heart could bear. What was I going to do? My commute was part of the job. One didn't exist without the other, and I couldn't just walk away. The work we were doing was so promising and, if we were successful, it would be life-changing for millions of patients and their families. I hugged my girls tightly, knowing I would have to bide my time.

Around that time, we lost our Lola. She had been having a hard time walking when we lived in California, and the vet had misdiagnosed her with a hip problem. It turned out to be her spine, so we took her to a specialist, but she was never the same. We tried everything to ease her discomfort, including acupuncture and physical therapy. Then she became incontinent and developed a terrible infection. The vet told us that she had been suffering. Doug and I were with her during her last breath. I held her tightly while Doug cried. She was my first little girl. She opened my heart to feeling a love that I didn't know was possible, a love that would continue to grow with Doug, our other dog Frodo, and then with our girls. How do you say goodbye to that? It was to be the first of many.

The realization that the girls had begun to notice my absence and wanted me, combined with the death of my beloved Lola, forced me to face hard questions: Could I have it all? Did I want it all? What did I actually want? I had everything I had dreamt of and worked so hard for, both professionally and personally. But the pace was too much. Something would suffer, and I didn't want anything to. In the back of my mind, I knew I needed to take control and start mapping a new life plan.

At the same time, the company was soon ready to make a move—and a bold one at that. We had three clinical trials going on at the same time and we decided to release the data from all of them simultaneously. This is rarely done because of how complicated the process is. Clinical trial data has the power to affect a company's stock price and is highly confidential because of the possibility of insider trading and corporate sabotage.

Matthew asked me to oversee the process. Our goal was to present the data at the J.P. Morgan Healthcare Conference held in San Francisco in January. It's the largest industry investment event of the year.

Before the holidays in December, I flew to Pennsylvania to make sure the unblinding of the data was being handled correctly. Then, on January 1, I headed to NYC to meet with Matthew and a very small group to review the unblinded data.

It was an unusually cold day in NYC. A polar vortex had blanketed the Eastern Seaboard, and we were sequestered in a law office for the entire week. The data from the clinical trial for the Alzheimer's drug wasn't what we had hoped for. The J.P. Morgan Healthcare Conference was less than a week away, and I had scheduled high-level meetings with more than thirty investors on the presumption that the data would be positive.

"How is everything?" Doug asked.

"Fine," I replied as normally as possible.

Even though I was talking to my husband, I couldn't reveal a hint of what was happening due to the sensitive nature of the data and its impact on the market. Conversations needed to be brief and limited. Suspicions of anything other than that would result in your phone being taken away, or worse. It was going to be a long week. Fortunately, we had the two other trials to consider. After much work and very little sleep, we issued our press release for the following Monday, which was also the first day of the conference. We confirmed our investor meetings and headed to JFK to catch our flight.

Then we received more bad news.

"What happened?" I asked Matthew, alarmed, as I returned from the ladies' room.

We were in the boarding area, and Matthew's expression told me that something had gone very wrong.

"You better speak to Nora," he replied angrily.

Nora was standing nearby on the phone, visibly upset. She was talking to the head of regulatory, and when I approached her, she quickly handed me the phone without looking at me. If things weren't great a week ago, they were even worse now.

Some of the data that we had been given was incorrect, and because of that, our press release contained incorrect trial data on the very first day of the largest and most significant health-care investment conference in the world. I was irate. How could this have happened? We had protocols in place to avoid something like this happening. Even though the person responsible for the error would be let go, we had to deal with the fallout now. There wasn't a lot of time to correct the situation.

"Should we even go to the conference?" Matthew asked.

He was right to ask. The conventional thinking would be not to show up, and most people would have canceled. However, I looked at this as a character-defining moment. People respected Matthew. He was a highly sought-after leader with a strong history and a long future ahead of him. How he handled this moment would speak volumes. We had less than twenty-four hours to turn things around.

"We have to go to the conference," I said. "We'll figure it out."

When they announced the pre-boarding of our flight, we were already on our phones, talking to a few key people and the lawyers. We got the information we needed to reissue the press release for the following morning and proceed with confidence, regardless of how uncomfortable it would be.

We needed to rethink Matthew's presentation and correct all of the slides. After we landed, we headed to his apartment and continued to work until one in the morning. Four hours later, I headed to the conference and switched out the slide deck so that the incorrect data wouldn't be presented.

The minute that people saw the press release, my phone started blowing up with texts and voicemails from colleagues and friends expressing their empathy and support. No one would ever want to be in the position we found ourselves in, but I knew that we had no other choice but to show up and face the music.

Matthew made his presentation, and, after the Q&A, we quickly headed to the hotel for our investor meetings. I had scheduled the meetings at a separate location to protect Matthew from running into people and being barraged by questions and conversations that would drain his much-needed focus and energy. We couldn't do anything about the data, but we could do everything about how we showed up. Many of the investors mentioned how surprised they were that Matthew hadn't canceled and that, instead, he had chosen to face the issue straight on when many other CEOs in his position wouldn't have.

A month and a half later, Matthew and a few of the board members decided to leave the company, and since I was brought in by Matthew, I would be exiting, as well. I immediately set about working with the executives and board on how to position their exit.

During this time, my girls were getting ready to start preschool. I was tired of commuting and missing the events of their daily lives. I wanted them to get to know their mommy, and I wanted to get to know them. Time was passing too quickly.

Doug had willingly and lovingly taken on the role of stay-at-home-dad, a role he excelled at and which brought him unparalleled joy and purpose. When I came home those weekends, it wasn't lost on me that the girls went to him and were closer to him than me. Rather than be jealous of it, I relished it. They were living a little girl's dream life with a doting, attentive daddy. I loved it, because I didn't have that. How wonderful their lives would turn out with his influence and attention.

But, I must admit, I did feel less comfortable with my own ability to parent. Doug was amazing at everything he tried: He read baby books, made homemade baby food, watched YouTube videos on how to do their hair, you name it. He was Super Dad. I, however, felt a bit insecure. But (and this is a big *but*) I did not think that I was like my mother. And Doug would always reassure me that I was a good mother; we just brought different things to the equation of being parents.

Our departure and the overall downsizing and restructuring were going to be announced on a Monday at a companywide town hall. The company told me that I needed to attend, even though I was leaving and there was no reason for me to be there. It was also the first day of preschool for my girls. I told the company that I couldn't. I had a more pressing engagement. I needed to take my girls to their first day of school. It's a day you never get back.

CHAPTER THIRTY-ONE

THROUGHOUT MY CAREER, I have been laser-focused on my work with many personal compromises along the way—compromises that involved my family. That focus had paid off financially, as I had negotiated generous compensation and exit packages to include a good salary, bonuses, equity, and continued health insurance—all of which was self-taught. Starting with my first job, when I began educating myself about finances and investments, taking the financial reins in my own hands paid off and allowed my family to live a financially secure and abundant life. With this being in place, I was looking forward to a self-imposed break.

The next six months were full of family time and recharging. One of my favorite parts of living in Dripping Springs was how family-oriented it was. The community prioritizes children and community parenting, and many of the restaurants and microbreweries offered playscapes for children. Doug and I would regularly take the girls to our favorite place in a neighboring town. The family-owned Shady Llama, which, in addition to the promised llamas and a few donkeys, had an outdoor beer and wine garden with live music and views of the best sunsets the Hill Country had to offer. We'd go there a few times a week and lie in the hammocks together or sit around the fire pits and chat with other families as live music played in the background.

Everyone brought their dogs, and it was a great place to meet friends, make new ones, and watch our girls play. In fact, this was one of the places where the girls learned to be social and meet and play with other kids and families. Instead of growing up isolated and staring out the window at the other kids playing, like I did, my girls laughed and played with the other kids. Instead of growing up afraid of dogs and being told that they were dirty, my girls learned how to approach other people's pups safely and play with them (and even pet a llama). Instead of being told to stay with their "own kind," our girls were encouraged to introduce themselves to others, and the Shady Llama provided a safe environment for that to happen. But, out of all the things they learned, perhaps my favorite was that they learned to appreciate sunsets while lying in the hammocks at the end of the day. These became some of my most treasured moments.

"Purple, orange, and fuchsia!" The girls would exclaim, pointing to the sky. Even today, they stop to appreciate beautiful sunsets.

∼

As wonderful as that community was, I was having a hard time finding "my people." Since I was often away traveling, the other moms would often say something along the lines of "Bless your heart, you are just like our husbands—always working!"

Even though a part of me loved it there, another part felt isolated and alone. I missed the diversity of New York City. In Dripping Springs at that time, you could count the people of color on one hand, and that number included me and my girls. When I dropped them off at school, they disappeared into a sea of children with blond hair and blue eyes. I didn't want the twins to feel like they were different or that they had to fit in somehow.

I also didn't want them to feel like a target, especially as issues around race, police shootings, and protests started to dominate the national news. I'll never forget driving past the neighborhood's one Black high school kid standing on a corner holding up a sign that said, "Ask me anything about being Black, I'm happy to speak with you."

As welcomed as we had felt as a family in this community, I knew that I wanted my girls to grow up with a variety of people and cultures. The world was changing but, in many ways, not fast enough. Austin had the reputation of being where San Francisco was fifteen years ago in terms of the biotech industry, but most of the local companies were smaller start-ups not quite ready to hire a senior executive at my salary. I also knew that I was becoming a bit of a unicorn in my industry, so it was unlikely that my next opportunity would come from a recruiter as it had earlier in my career. Instead, it would need to come from my network, and as science and business minded as I am, I also believe in karma. Doug would tease me about it, but I knew that the right opportunity would come along at exactly the right time, and it did.

Six months after I took my break, I was contacted by a company to work with them as a consultant. Word was spreading about my recent track record. Not long after, I was hired by another company to do the same. I was interested in nothing less than creating transformation and working with companies that wanted the same. I wasn't interested in keeping the trains running, I wanted to lay new track, and often that meant going into sticky and challenging situations and fixing them. I've never been drawn to doing things for the sake of doing things. I like high risk with high reward. I find it very gratifying to fix problems that other people can't. Perhaps it's because I was never able to fix my mom or even get her to see my point of view. She refused to change. She accepted the status quo, and that feels like death to me. Nothing illustrates that better than when my dad was in the hospital. Instead of accepting the fact that he wasn't getting the treatment that he deserved, I wrote a letter to the head of the hospital and his team so that everyone would see it, and it made a difference in how my dad was treated.

When it comes down to it, my job is to ensure success, and I'm going to do everything I can to accomplish that. My mother's job was to do that for me, but she failed miserably. It wouldn't be a stretch to say that I want others to succeed partly because I never received that.

I may not have gotten an MBA or law degree, but turns out, I didn't need them. I knew where the lines were from a legal and regulatory standpoint and could dig into all areas of a business to advise on strategy because of all my previous experiences. I could talk to employees, board members, investors, and analysts. I loved swooping into a company and, in a short but intense period, creating value. I thrived on working with urgency and passion with leaders who wanted to change the world and improve people's lives. Had I envisioned this when I was just starting? I didn't even know this possibility existed, and, at the time, it didn't. I created it.

My experience also taught me that I needed to feel strongly about the products and conditions they treated. I couldn't just work on anything for anybody. I needed the right partners—meaning the right CEO and the right board—and most of all, I needed to be trusted by them. They say hindsight is 20/20, but my vision forward had been just as clear, and even though I didn't know exactly what would happen next, I knew what I was looking for, which is half the battle. Soon, I would meet two men who would change the trajectory of my career.

CHAPTER THIRTY-TWO

"I NEED YOU TO work with us right away," said Craig, the CEO of a company that was working on the first product approved to treat peanut allergies—something I was very interested in because of being a parent and knowing what a serious issue it was. A colleague had referred me to him, and I only had about fifteen minutes to research his company before our call, but something struck me as odd.

"Why isn't your stock performing?" I asked.

Given the serious nature of food allergies—especially peanuts, which are the most likely to cause anaphylaxis and death, the company should have been doing better—much better.

"You got it right away!" he exclaimed. "That's exactly our problem."

We talked for half an hour more before he asked if I was available to start working with them. I liked Craig. He was direct and transparent, and we would be working on a product that could change the lives of millions of families. I was definitely available.

"We're in a state of crisis," he said. "Can you help me fix this?"

In less than a month, he was going to present at the J.P. Morgan Healthcare Conference—the same conference where I had helped Matthew through the data debacle. He sent me a contract that afternoon, and I started work immediately. It was December 13, 2018.

Looking through the investor deck and slides, I quickly identified their problem. Instead of telling a compelling story about their business, there were just slides and slides of data. This is a common mistake. Data is important, but it needs an engaging narrative to attract attention, and it's up to the company to tell it. During a presentation, you only have a finite amount of time to grab people's attention and take them on a journey to, ultimately, win them over. What is the company promising and why? Why should investors invest in you over someone else? I called Craig and gave him my feedback.

"Will you take a crack at it?" he asked.

I sat at the kitchen table for twelve hours straight, reworked the entire presentation, and sent it to him.

"You don't even know the business and you got it," he said. "This is exactly what I was looking for."

I joined him at the conference, where he unveiled the presentation that I had created. It felt gratifying to be there under very different circumstances than last time, but with a CEO that trusted me as much as Matthew had.

After the conference, Craig flew me to the company headquarters in Brisbane, California, and introduced me to his executive team, letting them know I'd be working with him on a few projects. When he asked me to look at what the VP of communications was doing, I did and then I made some recommendations. The VP wasn't thrilled about that.

"Stay in your lane!" she spat at me.

"Have you ever even done this before?" another one of the executives asked about an important FDA meeting.

"Yes," I responded, calmly. "Five times. Would you like to see my resume?"

In situations like these, I disengage from the hostility and focus on the goal. I'm well practiced at it because I've done it my entire life. One of the insidious ways my mother would criticize me was by doing it in Urdu when we were around other people, so no one could understand—all the while with a smile on her face, as if she were saying something sweet. This is why people, even my closest friend Lisa, would think my mom was nice. They didn't know what was really going on. A couple of execs were not going to ruffle my feathers. When Craig asked me about it, I tried to answer honestly yet diplomatically.

"I tried my best," I told him. "But they weren't receptive." The only way to succeed is by keeping focused on the goal instead of difficult personalities and getting mired in pettiness and negativity.

Within a month, Craig asked me to consider joining the company full-time. This wasn't a surprise to me. Consulting had been a great way for both of us to see if it would be a fit, and it was. Craig, like Matthew, is a big-picture thinker, which is why we worked so well together.

Later that month, I was spending two weeks in Australia with Doug on a Formula 1 trip when Craig called to ask if I could be on an hour-and-a-half call. I woke up at four in the morning Aussie time to join them. It was then that I realized how much I liked working with them. They were truly collaborative, and they valued my input. I accepted the role and joined the team officially in April.

When I arrived at my first board meeting, I found all the board members, including two female board directors, sitting at the conference room table with the male executive team members. However, the female executive team members, my colleagues, were sitting off to the side in chairs along the wall. I was surprised by this. Instead of joining them on the sidelines, I took a seat at the table and would continue to.

At every board meeting I went to after that, they always chose to sit on the side when our male counterparts would be at the table. It's not a stance I would recommend. It reminded me of the gender-segregated events from my childhood, where my mother would force me to sit with the women and girls, insisting, "That's the way things are." But her most cutting remark—one I had never forgotten—was "You're never going to be as good as a man." It felt like she was throwing down the gauntlet, and I'd always think in response: "Why not? I'll show you."

I think growing up in the patriarchal society of my parents' friends showed me the unjustness of expectations of women in society. I was never dainty or demure, nor am I now. I don't cook, sew, garden, or craft. Doug did all of that, though, and more. I was lucky he was such a Renaissance man. We each bring our own value to life, regardless of societal expectations. And because of my upbringing, it's important for me to continue to advocate for women not to succumb to stereotypes designed by men within a system architected by men.

Over the years, I would take quizzes about female and male work and personality traits, and I always checked most of the male traits' boxes. Maybe it's because I had rebelled against my mother's constant pushing and expectations, always saying that I would never be as good as a man. My response was that instead of trying to fit into any cultural or religious boxes or stereotypes, I would create my own.

~

With many executive positions, there are corporate goals attached to the role that affect the executive's bonus. There aren't usually corporate goals around communications, but, in this role, there were, which showed me how seriously the board took my work and that we were on the same page in viewing communications as a priority and using metrics to measure success—something I've always done. I would create my plan and use analytics to measure progress.

The three groups of industry influencers that we needed to focus our efforts on were physicians, investors, and advocacy/media groups, and it appeared that all of them had the same misinformation and were spreading it freely. I needed to change that, so I hit the road.

I called it my Repair Tour. For the next couple of months, I flew around the country with our medical director and met with all of the physicians who were mischaracterizing the product and the issue to the media. We respectfully and diplomatically provided the doctors with the correct information. No visit was too short or too far away. One afternoon, I flew from Austin to Stanford, California, for a quick half-hour meeting, and then got back on a plane and flew home. The

Repair Tour went to the root of the problem and fixed it. We corrected the narrative, and we did it proactively instead of reactively.

I was able to touch every aspect of the business, from legal to advocacy, and from pricing and compliance to affecting employee culture. This was the result of my insatiable desire to learn and be challenged, which gave me the experience and knowledge far exceeding the job title I started out with in the industry. It was a job that hadn't even existed. I created it. Instead of being trapped or pigeonholed, I was working with people who also wanted to change the landscape.

CHAPTER THIRTY-THREE

"SHE'S NOT GOING TO make it," said the nurse.

It was Friday evening. I had just come home from a business trip to New York and was putting my bags down in the kitchen when the phone rang. It was the nurse from my mother's adult living facility.

The last time I visited my mother was the previous year, and I had asked Lisa to come with me for moral support. I could always count on Lisa to be there for me. She was there when my father was dying, and she would be there for me now. Lisa and her mom gave me the love and support my mother couldn't or wouldn't.

Three years had passed since I told my mother that I needed a break from her, but the break didn't mean I never wanted to see her again. I just needed to control when and how often I saw her. It was about seeing her on my terms. Having that control allowed the relationship to be somewhat manageable.

When the twins entered my life, I started sending pictures of them to my mother and, occasionally, I'd leave messages for her. She never called me back. When the girls turned three, we called her, but it went to voicemail, so again, we left a message and, again, I never heard back.

So, the following June, when I was going to New York for another business trip, I called her to arrange a visit while I was there. The Sunday before my Monday flight to the East Coast, I left another message and again, I didn't hear back. On Friday evening, I arrived home from the trip, and that's when the nurse called me.

"Your mother has been very sick," the nurse said. "You need to come immediately."

"Dammit," I thought. "I was just there." I assumed that she was too sick to return my calls. I hung up and booked my flight for the following morning. I had dinner with my family, then went to bed without unpacking my suitcase.

When I arrived at her appointment, my mother was unconscious. I called Craig and let him know what was happening.

"Take whatever time you need," he said.

Then I called Lisa and told her what was happening.

"Where are you staying?" she asked. I hadn't even thought about that yet. "Come to the house," she said. "You can stay with me."

The next day, I sat with my mother as she lay in the bed motionless. In the Islamic tradition, before someone dies, you are supposed to whisper in their ear that you forgive them for all their sins and ask for forgiveness for your own. But did I forgive her? Could I say those words and mean them? And if I didn't say them, would I be robbing my mother of her dignity in death?

The nurse came in and checked on my mother. After she left, I pulled my seat a little closer to the bed and gazed at my mother's face. My mother had been my biggest detractor. Could I forgive her for doing everything in her power to diminish me and my life? To say that she wasn't equipped to be a parent would be putting it mildly. She was someone who probably shouldn't have had children. I knew that her life, in many ways, was unfulfilling, yet her lack of self-awareness and passivity always exasperated me. She refused to be anything other than who she was—even if it caused pain to those closest to her. I wondered if she would have been happier if she had stayed in India.

It was now evening, and the room had become dark. My mother's breath was quiet.

"I forgive you for all your sins," I whispered in her ear. "Do you forgive me for mine?"

I stayed at her bedside until she passed, a few days later. Per the religious requirements and my mother's wishes, there would be no viewing, and her body would be brought to the mosque for prayers. Then, she would be buried next to my father, and all of this needed to happen within twenty-four hours.

That night, I stayed with Stephanie, whom I'd now been friends with for decades, and, the following morning, I got up to get ready for my mother's funeral. Stephanie gave me one look.

"Stay right there," she said. "I'll be right back."

She ran to Dunkin' Donuts and got me a latte, then helped me put myself together—even touching up my hair to cover the few grays showing. When the car came to pick me up, I was finally ready—not because of the latte, or the touch-up, but because of the love and support that I felt from her and all my girlfriends, my soul sisters. Everyone, with very little notice, showed up. My friend Carrie dropped her kids off at school and then drove directly to the burial. Andrea was already on a train from Boston, and I would see Lisa and her mom shortly.

After the burial, I only had a short time before I needed to catch my flight, so my girlfriends and I went to lunch and had a cocktail. The next day I was back at work.

"What are you doing here?!" asked Craig.

Everyone grieves differently. With my dad, the grieving process took a long time. With my mother, the grieving happened a long time ago. There was nothing else to do or say.

"I need this," I told him. "This is how I do it."

That summer, I traveled extensively for work. The month that my mother passed, I was home for only three days, but I would talk to Doug and the girls every night. He was my rock. Commuting from Austin to the Bay Area wasn't ideal, so I rented myself a short-term apartment close to the office. After work, I would grab dinner at a neighborhood bar called Jack's and look for a temporary apartment big enough for the family until we found a permanent home back in California.

The housing market in the Bay Area was still intensely competitive. People with more resources than us were regularly being outbid. It was even worse than when we had bought our first home here years earlier. That house had sold within two hours of being listed, with multiple offers over our asking price. The buyers had been two engineers who worked at Facebook and Google, and we made a nice little profit that went toward our home in Dripping Springs—a home that was much bigger than what my real estate agent was now showing me. These homes were called jewel boxes because they were tiny and expensive and had no outdoor area to speak of. With the twins getting bigger, we would need more space.

"What about the East Bay?" I asked Doug.

Earlier that week, a colleague had invited me to her home for drinks. She lived in a gated community that had a new development tract under construction.

"I know it's not the neighborhood you were thinking of, but you should come take a look," she offered.

I met her at the community's hilltop clubhouse, and we sat on the patio overlooking the bay glistening in the distance. The sunset reminded me of Austin, and when I looked around the club, it was full of people of color. People who looked like me. It felt like I was finally home.

"When is the tract opening up?" I asked.

"The auction will be in May," she said.

Turns out, the auction was on Mother's Day. I would miss being with my family, but I bid for the house and got it. Afterward, I took myself out to brunch and called Doug and the twins.

"Mommy just bought you a house," Doug told the girls.

CHAPTER THIRTY-FOUR

THE LAST FEW YEARS had been a whirlwind, and I was looking forward to some stability and time with my family. My one-year anniversary working with Craig was in December 2019, and, come March, we'd be launching a new product. It was the first time in many years that I had been with a company that long. I was excited for what 2020 would bring.

That January, the board and executive team were discussing the financing for the upcoming product launch. I didn't agree with the strategy that the corporate financial officer, general counsel, and outside counsel wanted to take.

"Samina has a different opinion," the CFO said. "Let's hear what she has to say."

I laid out my case and, after some discussion, the board adopted my position. It felt extremely gratifying to be listened to and valued. My strategy turned out to be the right one, and I felt like I had broken through another barrier.

It was an extremely busy time. During the last days of January, we were given the green light by the FDA, and, six weeks later, on March 13, the first patient was given the first-ever approved treatment for peanut allergy. Three days later, on March 16, I headed to our offices for the analyst call where we would officially launch the product. It was the same day that Covid-19 was declared a national emergency—less than a decade after I had worked with U.S. government affairs on how to prepare for an eventual national pandemic. That time had come. After finishing up the workday, I left the office, never to return.

~

For most of my career, I kept my personal life separate from my work life, partly because I wanted to maintain a polished and professional image and partly because of my childhood. The pandemic ended that. Like many, I found myself sitting in my apartment, staring at my monitor on a video conference call with my family and our dog Frodo in the background. The girls had turned four and shared a bedroom, and now they would share a view into my work life, as well—at least until we moved into our new home, which wouldn't be finished for another few months.

To stay connected, we decided that each of us on the executive committee would create personal videos from our homes that would be shared with employees. It was the first time in the thirty-plus years of my career that I would let down my guard (from a work perspective) and invite people into my home. People loved it.

When I asked the girls if they wanted to be included, they jumped at the chance. Doug was the director and camera-man, since he was always so creative, and I wrote the script.

Even Frodo made a guest appearance. The connection that this created would help see us through what was to come.

On May 25, George Floyd was murdered by the police. Once again, it brought to light the mistreatment, inequity, and brutality many people of color face daily. The executive team wanted to discuss reaching out to our employees to express our dismay and support so, the next day, we got on Zoom to have a meeting about it.

"I want to be sensitive to the fact that we are a bunch of white people talking about this," said Craig, who is South African. Everyone nodded their heads in agreement.

"Umm . . . I'm not white," I said.

There was a pause and then everyone broke out in laughter at the realization that I was, in fact, not "white." So much for my mother's constant criticism that I would never fit in or be accepted—that I shouldn't even try because I would never "be one of them." Her "us" versus "them" view of the world was always so limited and one that I never experienced. Throughout my entire career, I never once thought about the fact that I wasn't white. It wasn't until that moment, when we were specifically discussing issues of race, that those words came to mind and out of my mouth. Along with another person on our team who had biracial children, I became the executive sponsor of our diversity, equity, and inclusion initiative.

It was a full-circle moment for me. I thought back on my childhood when my mother would say, "You can't," And I'd reply, "I can." Or when she would threaten, "You won't," and I'd say, "I will." And I did.

That August, the company was sold for $2.8 billion. By that point, I had played an integral part in four high-value acquisitions in less than a decade. The deal closed the following October, and I stayed on through December 2020 to help with the transition.

There were many full-circle moments during this time. When we finally moved into our new home, Doug and I enrolled the girls in a K–12 Christian private school. It was not only a top school, but it also had a diverse student body, so instead of being the only brown-skinned kids in the school, the girls would be two of many.

Given my background, it was ironic that the girls would be taking Bible study and learning about Jesus just as I had. Doug and I didn't consider ourselves religious in any way. We had liked the idea of community that church could offer, especially since Doug and I didn't come from large families, but since neither of us really believed in organized religion, that didn't seem to leave us a lot of options. Yet, it was on our minds, even when we lived in Pennsylvania and were first trying to have children. Because of that, when we first moved to California, we checked out a Unitarian church in Palo Alto. Everyone was very warm and welcoming—almost too much so. Perhaps it was because we were New Yorkers, but whatever the reason, we decided not to go back.

Fast forward to 2021: we were on a family road trip in our camper van, and our girls were singing at the top of their lungs songs they had learned about Jesus at their school.

"It's like a church revival in here," laughed Doug.

That winter, we went to Cabo San Lucas for Christmas. One of my girls saw a Nativity scene and ran up to it excitedly.

"I love Jesus!" she screamed.

Doug gave me a look.

"Samina Bari, what is going on here?" he asked, jokingly.

All parents confront tempering what their children learn in school with their own beliefs. My mother dealt with it by stubbornly and blindly insisting on her point of view without any explanation, which only fueled my skepticism, alienation, and rebellion. I wasn't about to make the same mistake with my kids. Instead, I wanted to expose them to a variety of different cultures and belief systems. Are Jesus and God a part of that? Yes, and so are Buddha, Allah, and Krishna.

One of the things we loved about living in California is the cultural diversity. We took the girls to Diwali, or the Festival of Lights, which is one of the major religious festivals in Indian religion. The colorful festivities full of music and dance and sweet treats thrilled them and fueled their natural curiosity and openness.

I try to look at every "why?" that the girls ask as a teachable moment. I want to give them the evidence, the science, and the facts, and then, ultimately, they are going to believe what they believe. I know that what they think and believe today isn't what they are necessarily going to believe when they're older, but they will know how to come to their own decisions instead of blindly accepting things at face value.

One afternoon, one of the girls and I were talking about someone who was having heart surgery.

"God will heal them," my daughter said.

"You can pray to God and that can help," I answered. "But if you were going to have an operation, doctors and medicine are what will make us better."

That's not to say that I'm not open to other ideas and modalities. Even with my background in bringing life-changing drugs to market, I'm usually the last person to take a pharmaceutical drug. In fact, much to Doug's dismay, I'm a huge believer in energy and natural remedies such as Ayurveda and Chinese medicine.

"But it's not FDA approved," he'd say.

He may have been right but, just the same, these remedies can work, so I've used them, which doesn't take away from the fact that medicine can radically improve people's lives. I've seen it firsthand from my early days at the hospital to today. Unfortunately, we're not at the point where medicine can heal everything or everyone. Our sweet little Frodo died that year. He had been a cancer survivor, and, like Lola, we had done everything for him, He had gone on to live a long full life, but finally it was his time. He died in our arms in our family home, and we still talk about him every day.

It's never easy to let go of those you love. It is particularly hard when it happens to someone at the peak of their life.

CHAPTER THIRTY-FIVE

"SAM," BEGAN LISA, THE only one who calls me that, "I have cancer." My body flushed as a surge of adrenalin coursed through it. I flooded her with questions. I wanted to know everything. I needed to know everything—then, maybe, I could help.

"Who is your doctor? Where are you going? You need to see the best oncologist, the best hospital, and the best treatment. Let me help. Let's stay in touch about this. I want to be in the loop." But, at the same time, I knew Lisa, and I wanted to respect her wishes.

"I know you're not going to want every conversation to be about this," I said. "So, we don't have to talk about it unless you want to." I hung up the phone and sank to the floor, sobbing because the cancer had metastasized.

"Why aren't you going to Sloan Kettering?" I had asked her.

She had chosen a hospital closer to her home. If I were there, I thought to myself, I would pick her up and drag her to the best hospitals, even if they were farther away. I thought about when she was pregnant with her first son, and we were both living in Staten Island. Her father was dying of a brain tumor, and she told me she was going to drive herself to NYU Medical Center. I wouldn't allow it.

"Absolutely not," I said. "Not in your condition."

Back then, I could insist that I would drive her, but now I was three thousand miles away.

"Let me come see you," I said. "I just want to spend time with you. Let me take care of you."

I booked a flight for July, but a week before my departure, she called me.

"I can't have a visit now," she said. "They scheduled me for another treatment. I'll see you at the wedding."

Her son, my godson, was getting married in October after postponing twice during Covid. Of course, I would be there. From July to October, Lisa was in and out of the hospital. The cancer had spread throughout her body. The last time I had seen her was at my mother's burial back in June and then, because of the pandemic, two years had gone by. As October approached, we talked about her son's wedding. She told me about her son and his fiancé's plans, the dress she was going to wear, and then she paused.

"I'm going to need a wheelchair," she said quietly.

Up until that point, we had been acting like everything was fine, even though, in my heart of hearts, I knew everything was very much not fine. I could hear the weakness in her voice, and I felt powerless and faraway.

The Saturday before the wedding, I heard the words I never wanted to hear.

"I'm going into hospice," she said in a strained whisper. "Thank you for being such a good friend. Thank you for loving me like a sister and for being a part of my life and my sons' lives." She made me promise that I wouldn't tell anyone that she was in hospice.

I was sitting on the floor in my closet with the door shut, tears streaming down my face. I could barely breathe.

"Please hold on," I managed. "Please let me see you."

I didn't know if the wedding was still going to happen, but, either way, I had to see her.

"I will never love anyone like I love you," I said. "Please, Lisa. Please, wait for me to get there."

"We'll see," she said faintly. "I won't be able to go to the wedding."

As soon as I got off the phone, I called her son. I couldn't imagine how they were going to have a wedding without her.

"I don't know what's going on, but I'm coming," I said in a message.

I had known Lisa for fifty years. I needed to see her. Since her son was her primary point of care, I would need to coordinate whatever my plans were with him. It sounded like the wedding was still moving forward, so my plan was to fly out Thursday morning. The following Wednesday, her son called and said they were canceling the wedding.

"Come anyway," he said. "Mom wants to see you, so come straight to the hospital."

When I arrived at the hospital, I joined her son, who told me she was still conscious. I quietly entered the room and held her hand. Tears streamed down her face as we talked and cried together.

"I will take care of your boys," I promised. "You don't have to worry about anything." She whispered, "Thank you."

Closure is a hard thing to come by in times like these. How

do you say goodbye to someone who knows you better than anyone? She was more than a friend. She was my sister. She knew me, warts and all, and accepted and loved me anyway. When my mother tore me down, Lisa would build me up. She gave me confidence when I couldn't find any. She shared her family with me, and her family became my family. Her parents became my parents. Her children were my children. Distance hadn't changed that. Careers hadn't changed that. Time hadn't changed that.

The next morning, after her sons, mother, sister, and I said our tearful goodbyes, we stepped into the hallway to give her the grace to pass, and, a few minutes later, she was gone. I would feel lost without her for years to come.

The memorial was the following Wednesday. I had only packed a few clothes, so Stephanie picked me up and took me shopping for socks and other necessities to get me through the extended stay. We kept the memorial small, only inviting close friends and family. It was bittersweet, but everything Lisa would have wanted.

The following weekend, Andrea, Stephanie, and I had planned to go on a weekend getaway to the Jersey Shore. We had made the plans long before I knew what was happening with Lisa. After being at the Days Inn for the week going back and forth to Lisa's house, I thought it would be a good idea to stick with the plan. I needed to decompress and have space to cry.

Her son and his fiancé eloped, and they now have a daughter. After remodeling the family home that they grew up in (much the same way that I had with Lisa and her parents) they've moved in and are building their own family and memories. It's poignant to watch this knowing that Lisa never got to meet her granddaughter. She would be proud of her boys, who are now successful young men creating their lives out of the love she generously and effortlessly shared. My twins consider her sons their cousins.

~

It's often said that blood is thicker than water, but the full quote is actually "the blood of the covenant is thicker than the water of the womb," meaning that the relationships we choose are often more meaningful than the ones we are born into. This was certainly true when it came to the love I received from Lisa and her mom, as well as her boys and their families. The same goes for Doug, our dogs, my tribe of girlfriends and their families, and the hilltop community in which we lived. I may not have found my church, but I found my people and made my own family, my Chosen Family. And then, my world collapsed.

CHAPTER THIRTY-SIX

THE GIRLS HAD JUST celebrated their seventh birthday with a massive party at our house. We had a taco truck, and Doug made big batches of margaritas along with his famous carrot juice mescal cocktail. With an open-door policy, our house had always been a gathering place for everyone in the community, and that day was no exception. Everyone was there. It was the polar opposite of how both I and Doug had grown up, which is probably why we understood each other so well. Everything we didn't have when we were children, we wanted to provide to our girls. Because of that, they were surrounded by a community that loved them, and they were thriving. As we watched our girls play, Doug and I looked at each other and smiled. We were proud and excited— proud of our girls and excited to be entering a new phase of our marriage.

After struggling so long with IVF and the heartbreak of multiple miscarriages that inevitably put a strain on our marriage, we finally had the family that both of us wanted (even if Doug didn't know it when we first met). The days of relocating for my work were over. I could be picky about whatever new position I took, and, because of my successes, was attracting consulting work that felt professionally satisfying. We had built our forever home and created our forever family. We had everything we always wanted, and none of it had come easily.

I think back to the little girl trapped in her childhood bedroom, lying on her twin bed consumed with loneliness and rage while listening to love songs on the radio. I think back on how desperately I hoped and dreamed that someone could love me as deeply as those songs, but how afraid I was that it would never happen—that I was, perhaps, unlovable. I never felt it from my mother, and I only became close to my dad as an adult. My life had felt like a battle against a mother that tried to destroy the very essence of who I was. She would smile to her friends and then, behind their backs, snarl at me saying, "You'll never be good enough."

Everything I wanted to do, she'd threaten, "Do not!" Every tradition that I went against, she'd respond, "You will not." Every time I listened to my heart and desires, she'd scream, "You cannot!" But I could, I would, and I did. And what did I have to show for it? Everything. Doug gave me the love that I always wanted and needed. He filled the many holes in my heart. Sometimes he'd say, "I don't know if you know how much I love you." But I did. I felt it to my core.

Following the girls' birthday was spring break, so we drove to Southern California and stayed at the Great Wolf Lodge with its 105,000-square-foot indoor water park, movie theater, bowling alley, and multiple restaurants. After a full day of activities, we'd put the girls to bed, and Doug and I would stay up late talking. We could always talk about anything, not just as husband and wife, but as best friends.

One of our friends at the time was having open-heart surgery, and he had told his wife that if anything happened to him, he wanted his ashes scattered at the Formula One race-track in Belgium called the Circuit de Spa-Francorchamps, or Spa for short. I couldn't help but laugh, imagining that his wife mustn't have been too pleased about that.

"Where are you going to put my ashes? Next to Lola and Frodo?" Doug laughingly asked. "I would want to be in the places that I enjoyed the most."

Even though we had discussed all the necessary (and unimaginable) end-of-life details that parents do when they have children, it wasn't something I really wanted to think about or get into too much detail about. He grabbed my hand and switched the conversation to our upcoming wedding anniversary.

"Let's go to Cabo," Doug said. "Just you and me." It would be our sixteenth wedding anniversary, and now that the girls were a little older, we were starting to plan little getaways together. We had even started going on date nights again. It reminded me of when we first met. We would go to Cabo every Christmas and zip away on impromptu, surprise vacations.

When we arrived home and were approaching our driveway, Elle proclaimed, "I love our house. I want to live here with you forever." I turned to her and smiled, as my heart filled with joy. It was a perfect moment after a perfect week.

The next day, the adventures continued. Doug and the girls had been watching YouTube shows featuring every creepy crawly creature you could imagine, and Doug wanted to build the girls a terrarium, so we drove into Berkeley and checked out a few reptile stores. After a couple hours, we stopped for lunch at a cute place in Sausalito and then decided to visit the zoo on the way home. It was another perfect day.

The next day Doug and I were planning on joining our friends in the city to see the San Francisco Giants play their season-opening game. Doug had arranged for a sitter to take the girls overnight and booked a room for us at the Four Seasons, along with dinner reservations and massages. It was going to be a romantic weekend alone after a fun-filled week with the girls.

That night after the zoo, we all showered and changed, and Doug got dinner prepared. As we were just about to sit down to eat, he received a couple texts from his friends who were having drinks at the neighborhood clubhouse.

"Would you mind if I joined them?" he asked. For a quick second, a part of me didn't want him to go, but then I thought again. We had such a great week together and would be together the following day and night. "Of course," I said. "Have fun!"

After dinner, I put the girls to bed, and went upstairs and settled into bed with a glass of wine to read. It was late and Doug wasn't home yet, but I didn't think anything of it because he and his friends would often hang out late together. I turned the page of my book, as I sipped some white wine, and snuggled under the blanket when the phone rang. It was my friend Serena, which was unusual because we normally just text one another

"Hey, is Doug home?" she asked. She went on to say that her husband had gotten home a while ago and she saw that our garage door was still open. Then she added, "there's an ambulance outside."

Something inside me knew it was bad. I ran out of the house in a panic and raced down the road toward the flashing lights of the ambulance, frantically yelling Doug's name. When I finally got there, the first thing I saw was the bottom of Doug's shoes. He looked like he was sleeping. So handsome and peaceful. But no. I started begging him to wake up. Begging him not to leave. Begging him for the kids, for me, for us. I was shaking, and someone threw a sweater around my shoulders. I shrugged it off. I wasn't cold. I was in shock.

The paramedic asked me what medicines he was taking, and I thought that maybe he had suffered a heart attack. His family has a history of heart disease. But then I saw the electric scooter. He hadn't driven to the clubhouse. He had taken his scooter. I had always hated that scooter. I became hysterical, asking, "What happened?! Somebody tell me what happened!"

A neighbor explained that someone driving home saw him lying in the street and called the ambulance. I realized that he had been lying there for a while. I was horrified. I was both sobbing and not sobbing. The paramedics tried to resuscitate him and couldn't. I knew that wasn't good. The brain can't survive that long without oxygen. We needed to get him to the hospital.

I asked my friend to take care of the girls. She called the girls' nanny, who came early and would keep them overnight as we had planned earlier. Meanwhile, the paramedics wouldn't allow me to ride in the ambulance with Doug, so I jumped in the fire commander's truck. Time became a blur. The next thing I knew, I was sitting in the waiting room of the ER, trying to calm myself down. I rationalized that if this was a cardiac event, then I would fix it. I would take care of him. I would make sure he ate more healthfully. I would do whatever was needed. I would take care of it and make him better. I could fix it like I had fixed so many things.

Finally, the doctors came, and I asked them about surgery. They just shook their heads. They said that Doug had a traumatic head injury, and that surgery wouldn't help. I couldn't believe them, so I made them show me the X-ray. I wish I hadn't. They took me to Doug's room, and I held his hand, kissed him and lay with my head on his chest for hours. His eyes wouldn't respond to the doctor's tests, and there wasn't any motor activity. They kept coming in to poke and prod him until finally I begged them to stop.

"Just make sure he's not in any pain," I cried.

"Do you have anyone you can call?" they asked.

I knew he wouldn't want anyone to see him like this, so I waited alone knowing that I was watching the person I loved the most in the world leave me forever. Having been with Lisa and both of my parents when they took their last breaths, I knew that he was aware of what was going on, so I played videos of the girls so he could hear their voices one last time. I told him how much I loved him, that I would always love him, and that he would always be the most amazing husband and father in the world. The nurses came in and told me I should go home to rest, but I wouldn't leave him.

At 3:30 in the morning, I called my friend Stephanie in New York, knowing that it was 6:30 her time and she'd be waking up. Then I called his mother, who also lived on the East Coast. After I got off the phone, I stayed with him until he took his last breath. Sometime later, I texted my friends from the neighborhood to pick me up.

They came right away. When we got to the house, my friends and I just sat in silence and cried. Word spread and I started getting calls and texts from all over the world. Our neighborhood was so close-knit that instead of the western convention of waiting to pay your condolences, people just came over. The door kept opening and closing all day long as friends streamed in. Everyone knew Doug and loved him. Many of them had seen him the night before at the clubhouse. People mentioned what a good mood he had been in, that he had stopped by everyone's tables and said hello. Nobody could believe that he was suddenly gone. Every single person, both women and men, was utterly broken and in tears.

That afternoon, Stephanie arrived. She had stopped everything when I called at 6:30 in the morning (her time) and was in my house by 2:30 Pacific time. She wrapped her arms around me, and I cried some more. My thoughts went to the girls, who were still at the babysitter's and weren't scheduled to come home until the next day. I wondered if I should tell them now, but I couldn't shatter their worlds just yet. I wanted them to have one last day of happiness.

The next day, when the babysitter brought them home, they were in such good moods. Then they saw all our friends at the house and asked what was going on. Suddenly, Elle looked at me and said, "Where's Daddy?" I took them upstairs to their bedroom and sat them down. Through my tears, I told them what happened.

Lily, who is quite similar to me, immediately went into fix-it mode. "What are we going to eat?" she asked. "You can't cook. We're going to starve." Elle fell into a pool of tears. "Daddy was my everything," she said. My heart broke once again. I held them as we all cried together.

"Does everybody know?" Lily asked. "Is that why they're here?"

I nodded. "You don't have to talk to anyone or do anything you don't want to do," I told them. "Just take your time. People are here for you, but if you don't want to talk to them, you don't have to." When we walked out of the bedroom, they went up to their babysitter first.

"Did you know?" they asked her. She just nodded through her tears. I could see they were dismayed by that knowledge. Lily turned away and went to the kitchen to start making a recipe for ratatouille. Elle sat down and started writing letters to her daddy. I began to question whether allowing them that final day of happiness was the right thing to do. I would soon have to address their distrust and fear that began to develop over the next few days and months. They were forever changed, as was I.

CHAPTER THIRTY-SEVEN

THEY CALL IT GRIEF brain—the inability to think or even function, and even though grief is not classified as a mental illness, it should be. Traumatic grief, which is what I was experiencing, led to diagnoses of PTSD, anxiety, and depression. Prescription bottles littered my bathroom counter. Getting out of bed was nearly impossible. I suffered from insomnia, or I would sleep all day. I couldn't remember if I had eaten and I usually forgot to. I lost weight and looked almost skeletal. My days were spent sitting in my house or lying in bed crying. I wasn't able to leave the house, and I certainly couldn't drive. I literally forgot how to operate a car and had no spatial awareness or even awareness of time.

If it hadn't been for my friends and community, I don't know what I would have done. Everything I had done for Lisa and my parents when they died, I was incapable of doing now for myself, or for Doug. I was on tranquilizers and felt like a zombie, more from the grief than the medication. As our wedding anniversary was approaching, I was filled with dread. I knew I didn't want to spend it alone. I decided that that would be the day for his memorial instead.

Doug never liked funerals. He preferred Irish wakes, with their sharing of stories and drinks. Whenever we'd see one depicted on TV, he'd say, "That's the way to do it." He would want his friends to laugh and drink and remember all the good times they had together, and, since he had been in the Marines, he would also receive a Marine Honor Guard ceremony.

My friends Abby and Sarena and our clubhouse management organized the service beautifully and thoughtfully. Over 120 people attended from all over the world. There were even remembrances for him in Japan, where he had worked and made lifelong friends, as well as in Germany. Doug used to say that no one would come to his funeral, especially after he saw the hundreds of people that came to honor my dad when he died. Doug had been deeply touched by that. "I've never made that kind of an impact on anyone," he said. Even when I listed all of his friends, he'd say, "yeah, but they live across the country," or "we don't really see them anymore." He had no idea how many lives he had touched, and they all came to honor him. Everyone shared stories, contributed pictures, and even created a beautiful video tribute to him. I have never witnessed so many adults, including men, cry the way they did for Doug.

I asked the girls if they wanted to speak at Daddy's service, and they didn't hesitate to say yes. Elle insisted on speaking first and opening the service with a message she had written for her daddy. I delivered my remarks as if in a blur through tears, and then Lily ended with a prayer that she had written herself for her daddy. Then the U.S. Marines began their Funeral Honors ceremony, and there wasn't a dry eye in the crowd. The girls handled it all remarkably well, although I could tell Lily was compartmentalizing her feelings. She told my friend Stephanie that she wouldn't cry. "Daddy wouldn't want me to cry," she said. And whenever anyone talked about Doug, she'd say, "Shhh! Don't say his name."

I had the girls begin grief therapy two weeks after he passed. I went to therapy as well, and, in time, I had all of us join a grief support group, one for children who had lost a parent and one for the parents. It was about the only thing I could do besides crying and being in bed. Since I couldn't drive, a dear friend would drive an hour every week to take me and the kids to therapy, and then she'd make us dinner and spend the night. She did that for months. Sometimes she'd take the girls for a weekend so I could just wallow and cry. Another friend, who was a retired schoolteacher, volunteered to tutor the girls every Wednesday evening.

Our community created a meal train and dropped off dinners since I didn't cook (and wouldn't have been able to even if I did). Other friends would fly in from their homes in Boston, New York, or New Jersey to spend time with me and the kids. They say it takes a village to raise children, and that village is even more needed when a parent suddenly dies.

That summer, Doug had planned to take us to Germany for the first time. He fell in love with the country when he had spent time there with his many Formula 1 races. "Daddy won't be able to go to Europe with us," said one of the girls. I hadn't thought we would go, but then I realized that they were expecting it, and I knew I needed to deliver. I needed to give them new memories, so, once again, my friends rallied and took over the planning of the trip. They handled all the arrangements: getting to the airport, arriving in Frankfurt, going to France, and getting back again. It was like I was a fragile piece of glass that was carefully handled from point A to point B.

While there, we had planned on meeting the family of an au pair we had wanted to hire before Covid hit. During the pandemic, we stayed in touch and all became close Covid friends. We even dedicated a room to her called Mona's Room, and, as soon as the restrictions were lifted, she came to visit us. A little later, Doug met her family during a trip to Germany. This was supposed to be the trip for all of us to meet them, but, instead, it would just be me and the girls. Her family graciously hosted us, and, afterward, the girls and I, along with friends from London, stayed in a beautiful chateau in Provence that Doug had selected.

When we arrived home, I had a new sense of clarity. My brain fog lifted somewhat, and I was finally able to drive. Years before, my focus had been on my career and making sure my family was financially secure. Now my focus was on the girls and making sure they were okay. I'm not sure what would have happened if I didn't have them.

I used to think the girls were so lucky because they had the best dad a girl could have and, because of that, they would grow up feeling loved, secure in their attachments, and confident in standing up for themselves. I constantly told Doug that he was a better parent than I was. He was more empathetic, compassionate, and patient. He used every moment as a teaching moment. Whereas I am serious and analytical, he was silly, fun, and creative. He would do crafts with them, take them camping, and cook with them. He did all these amazing things that I would never have thought of because I hadn't been exposed to them growing up.

Now, I constantly wonder if I'm doing the right thing. I worry about the long-term consequences of such a sudden and tragic loss. Every night, they crawl into bed with me. Sometimes, they cry because they didn't get to say good night to him that last night or tell him that they loved him before he died.

"He knows you love him," I told them. We made it a habit to express our love to the girls and each other, and the girls heard it and said it often. But now, as they huddle in bed with me, fear has crept into their hearts, and sleep has become elusive. They became afraid to fall asleep because their daddy died when they were sleeping, and so, instead, they became protective and hypervigilant. "Mommy, you're our only parent," they'd say. "What if someone comes to hurt you?" To comfort them, I had an alarm system with security cameras installed, and, every night, I'd show them how I was arming the house. I also ripped out all of the tall shrubbery in front of the house and put in lighting and low-lying land-scaping. As much as I've done to make them feel safe, they still sleep with me. Perhaps it's because they want to sleep on their daddy's side of the bed.

Wherever I go, they want to come. Once, I tried to go on an overnight trip and they became irate. "No nonsense trips!" they demanded. I tried to tell them that a happy Mommy is a better Mommy, but, in their eyes, the only reasonable trip for me to take is for work.

People often asked if we were going to move out of our home, thinking that somehow it would help with the grief, but how could we? The girls love the house, and our community means the world to us. The tragedy would be with us wherever we were. Instead, I started to make little changes around the house. I changed the rug in the girls' loft and gave them new side tables. Doug had been in the process of transforming his office, so I transformed it for him, adding all of his favorite things.

The following fall, the girls continued with school. They had, in fact, chosen to go back to school the Monday after Doug died. But soon their school, which was Christian, became problematic. In no time, the girls were coming home saying they wanted to be very good so they could go to heaven to be with Daddy. Despite my immobilizing despair, I dragged myself to the school and told them to stop describing heaven as a reward for good behavior. To the school's credit, they understood where I was coming from, but I knew that as soon as I could muster it, I needed to make a change. Even before Doug died, we were planning on changing schools, especially when we saw the girls coming home from first grade with forty-five minutes of homework. Academics are important, but not to the detriment of childhood development.

Yet, with everything that had happened, changing schools felt like a tall order when I couldn't even get out of bed. That was until they started coming home angry, frustrated, and just plain ornery. We would all end up fighting, which we had never done before, and it was so upsetting. Until I found out why. Then I became even more upset.

The girls told me that their school would start every day with a prayer for them, Doug, and me. So, every morning, they were being reminded that their dad was dead and that they were different from everyone else. No wonder they were emotional. I knew that the school had good intentions and didn't mean to trigger them, but I quickly put an end to that. I would need to take action sooner than I thought.

I reached out to the school that Doug and I were interested in before his accident. I was hopeful that this change would be good for them. Instead, it was the opposite. Typically, schools offer a "shadow day," where kids can visit and see what it's like. Unfortunately, this school had misrepresented what their shadow day was, so instead of being a day of visiting classes, the girls were subjected to three hours of tests. They cried throughout the whole thing, and, of course, the school rejected them. I was so upset by the school's poor communication and the fear that I had retraumatized them. I started to consider homeschooling, but how would I manage that? Every ounce of my body was filled with the fear that, without Doug by my side, I was ruining the girls' lives.

I decided to try the school again and worked with the girls' therapists to get them ready, but the girls were adamant. They didn't want to go, and Elle would say daily how much she hated math and school in general. It frightened me that she felt that way about education at such a young age. Finally, my friend Stephanie suggested Montessori, which I had thought was only for preschool.

After checking it out, I set the girls up for three shadow days, and they loved it. On one of the days, Elle was working with a teacher on a project and having a great time. The teacher looked at her and said, "this is math," and then added, smiling, "we're going to have fun." Now they both love school, and Elle even likes math. It has been a huge relief.

The other relief was providing the girls with the perfect au pair. After interviewing people and not finding the right match, I decided to reach out to Mona on the off chance that she would still be available. Much to my surprise, she was. The girls love her, and she has become a part of the family. Both the therapist and psychiatrist said that it was probably one of the best things that could have happened during this horribly tumultuous year.

The triggers are the one thing we haven't been able to avoid. Whether it's a song on the radio or a place we used to go, they are everywhere. I can no longer walk to the club-house because of what happened on that street. It took me months before I could even visit the clubhouse after the service.

The other unavoidable triggers are holidays. Father's Day was the worst, and then came my birthday, which I just wanted to ignore. I didn't even tell the girls about it, and asked a friend to take them so I could just be alone and cry. People offered to come by, but I just wanted the day to go away and ended up drowning my sorrows with two bottles of wine. It was the antithesis of the year before, when Doug surprised me by making a seven-course meal of all my favorite foods, complete with wine pairings. Lily acted as his sous chef while Elle played hostess. They set the table, designed menus, and hired a pianist to play. Doug even created a video that he played for me to celebrate our twenty-one years together. He always made me feel so special and loved, and now I was alone. It was unfathomable.

The next hurdle was Christmas Eve, which is when Doug had proposed, and, after that, New Year's. I couldn't have cared less about ringing in the new year. I decided, instead, that the girls and I needed to go away, so we visited a friend's family in Santiago, Chile. What I didn't realize was how dif-ficult it would be for the girls to see an intact family. Lily started to lash out and misbehave. I kept apologizing to my friends until I realized what was happening. Her denial over the last nine months was finally beginning to crack. She just couldn't keep it in anymore. With trauma and grief, nothing is as it seems. Acting out wasn't just acting out, and a tantrum wasn't just a tantrum. It was grief and rage pouring out of them. It underscored everything we did. Lily finally started to process her feelings and talk about missing her daddy. She would get angry and slam doors, and there were times I felt so helpless and worried but also relieved that it was finally coming out.

When we came back from that experience, whatever clarity I gained from our previous European trip was erased. It hit me hard that Doug and I would never spend another New Year's together, and that every year ahead of me was going to be without him. I spent the month of January in bed. Since then, I've tried to move forward as much as possible. I'm planning vacations and more travel with the girls because it's something that Doug and I loved so much. Every time we took a trip, we would bring back local artwork and hang it in the house, so now, when the girls and I go somewhere, we continue that tradition.

Other things are proving harder to do—even small things. I used to always complain about doing laundry, but there was a part of me that found it soothing. I knew my family was in the house, and it comforted me. Now, I can no longer fold laundry. I struggled to make myself pay bills and do the basic family accounting because I just didn't have the mental bandwidth. On top of that, the amount of administrative work involved in a spouse's death is outrageous. I've had to send out Doug's death certificate dozens of times, and, each time, it brings me back to his loss. This doesn't help with the grief or the rage, and, if anything, the injustice of the situation just compounds it.

My therapist tells me that I need more time to myself and that I need to find ways to lose myself and relax. I've been able to go off all the medications, but I'm not happy. There is no more true joy in my life. I think of Doug from the minute my eyes open after a fitful night's sleep, to a million times throughout the day, to my last thought at night. Elle said it best when she said, "I may look happy, but I am always sad."

One of the things I've learned is that not all grief is the same and not all people process grief in the same way. Complex traumatic grief is one of the most difficult forms of grief to navigate, and even though grief and loss are universally shared, we, as a society, are ill-equipped to handle it. We don't know how to speak about it or what to do with it. Often, we just want to fix or dismiss. Grief is a topic that no one is comfortable with. I am fortunate to have a community of friends that rallied around me, yet I was often taken aback by people's well-meaning but misguided comments.

"I know what you're going through," said one person. "I just lost my mother." That was not helpful, regardless of intention. The sudden loss of a spouse is nothing like the loss of an aging parent, which is an expected and natural part of the life cycle. It's understandable that people try to relate, but it ends up being alienating and dismissive.

"You're going to thrive," said another, trying to comfort me. "You're going to be fine after you get through all of this." Again, I didn't find that helpful, because the truth is, I'm never going to be the person that I was. How could I? A part of me died when Doug died. The author Megan Devine says it perfectly in her book, *It's Ok that You're Not Ok*: There is no silver lining around traumatic grief. It's horrifyingly painful and senseless, and you can't just wrap a pretty little ribbon around it and call it a gift.

"You're not going to be single for long," said another, as if dating or remarrying was anything I wanted to do. I still wear my wedding ring. Doug is still my husband, and I am still his wife. We were not divorced or separated. He died.

"Grief becomes you!" was another unfathomable comment I heard after I managed to drag myself out of bed and put on some moisturizer. "You're actually glowing," they added. These comments only made me feel more alone and isolated, and angry at how insensitive people can be. Of course, I realize that people mean well and they're just trying to fix something that they can't appreciate or understand.

After the initial outpouring of support faded away, receiving a text that said, "I'm thinking about you," let me know that I was not alone and forgotten. When people asked, "what can I do for you?" I was mute. It was too general of a question. I could barely think, so I was grateful for friends and neighbors who would just bring food or take the girls for the weekend or afternoon.

Many of the widows in my grief support group talk about how they used to be part of a friend group, but now that their spouse has passed away, they no longer receive invitations. I am incredibly fortunate to not have experienced this. Our friends still come over to our house for dinners and drinks, and I am still part of the broader group. I am invited to everything and am beginning to do the events that Doug loved to host, such as the Japanese Grand Prix or his whiskey and cigar nights. Now I host them in his honor.

I've also honored his wish to have his ashes spread in all the places he loved around the world. There's a part of him here in our home, and I've set aside ashes for the girls to scatter when they are old enough. That's the only future that I can see at the moment. They say that trauma inhibits one's ability to plan for the future, that's definitely true for me. Where I used to live for my twenty-year plan, now I live for the girls. I live to get through another day.

CHAPTER THIRTY-EIGHT

DID I KNOW THIS was going to be the last chapter of my book when I started? Not at all. The night that Doug had his accident, I was reading a draft of this manuscript, and Doug was planning on reading it that weekend. I couldn't wait to share this story with him. Of course, he already knew most of it. He knew how hard I had worked to create the life of my dreams with the family and love that I so desperately needed and craved as a child. Today, with Doug gone, a part of me has died. Doug was my other half, cleaved off violently in the night, never to return.

So who am I now?

All my life, I did everything I could to stuff my emotions or compartmentalize them. I had to. It's how I survived. After the childhood incident with my uncle and the subsequent betrayal of my mother, I shut down my heart for good. It was locked and I had thrown away the key. Who needs it? Doug taught me that I needed it.

I was better because of him. Spontaneous and playful. He pushed me out of my comfort zone, in large and small ways.

One time, while we were vacationing in Cabo, we were at a karaoke bar because he loved to sing, whereas I was much more reserved. I knew how much it would mean to him, so I worked up the courage to go on stage and sang *Come Sail Away* by Styx, which was a special song to us. Tears streamed down his face. How lucky I was to find this man.

Doug unlocked a level of love inside me that I didn't even know I had. His love helped heal me from the past and from the anger and resentment that had fueled my life. It didn't happen overnight. We both came from families with a narcissistic parent, so we knew we'd have work to do, and we did it. With Doug, I finally became the person I was meant to be. I loved being that person. She was loved and she loved back. With Doug gone, I look in the mirror and struggle to recognize the person staring back at me.

What I do know is that I am no longer defined by my career or my pursuit for success. I am no longer fueled by the anger that I had toward my mother. If anything, I probably wouldn't be the mother I am without her—which is not the same as saying that I am grateful for her. It could have been much worse. I could have ended up depressed, anxious, broken, or addicted to something to dull the pain—a shell of a person. In fact, there were moments, days, and weeks as a child when that's exactly how I felt. Luckily for me, I found escape and resilience in my close friends, school, and my dreams for the future. Not every child does.

Some people say that when you become a mother you have more compassion for your own mother. Do I feel compassion toward my mother? I understand that she struggled with lifelong depression. I understand the generational and religious influences that contributed to shaping who she was. I understand that she struggled to be a mother to me. Because of how she was as my mother, I vowed to be an entirely different kind of parent to my own children. One who would love and protect her children. One who would support them and give them the security, acceptance, respect and unconditional love that I never got. I checked off all the things I would never do, the things that my mother did to me. I was a better mother despite her, but, when it came down to it, it was because of Doug's ability to support me, heal my childhood wounds, and love me for who I truly am.

Throughout my life, I have experienced many full-circle moments, some that felt like a triumph, and some more poignant. But, with the loss of Doug, I found myself confronted with a full-circle moment that felt like a knife through my heart. My daughters had just come home from school and were standing in the doorway of my bedroom.

"Mommy, why are you always in bed?" they asked.

I was thrown back to my childhood standing at my mother's door, wondering if she would ever get out of bed, wondering how many days she would spend lying there in the dark, and the memory crushed me. I willed myself to speak. "Girls, I am just so sad about your daddy. I miss him so much. My heart, mind, and body need to be in bed." Even though the situation felt similar, I knew that it was different, and the difference was that I cared. I cared so much it hurt. My mother could not, would not, and did not care for me. Yet here I was, spending all day in bed, for days and months on end. I was powerless and immobilized by the grief that consumed me. I physically, spiritually, and mentally could not do the things I had done before. My resilience was snuffed out by the grief. I needed time, and I was afraid that if I didn't take that time, and didn't allow myself to feel, it would come out another way, which would hurt me and my children in the long run. I knew this from experience, because that's exactly what I had done as a child. I had stuffed my tears and the feelings of hurt and betrayal and was subsequently riddled with anxiety throughout much of my early adult life, regardless of the years of therapy and Prozac. I didn't want that for me, and I certainly didn't want that for my girls. I had to model a different way of being in the most devastating of circumstances.

"It won't always be like this," I reassured them. "I can give you hugs, but I just can't do everything right now."

Fortunately, Doug and I had built the loving and generous Chosen Family that now surrounded us. If my intent in writing this book was to tell you not to let your anger or other people's limited view of you destroy you, but, instead, to use it as fuel, then please know this: your Chosen Family and community are other sources of fuel, and it is never too late to create them. Despite everything we did to protect our girls, we couldn't protect them from this heartbreak. Thankfully, what we did do was surround them with people who loved them and would be there for them when life inevitably happens, when getting out of bed isn't an option, and when everything you think you know is unfathomable and rendered mute. I wouldn't be here today if it weren't for the people I love most and who love me back, and what makes the bond especially precious is that they don't have to. They choose to, and isn't that what life is all about? The choices we make, what we do with what is given to us, how we show up, and what we create for ourselves? At least, that's what I thought, but it's so much more.

Now I am intimately aware of how much I am powerless over, when there is no choice. I had no choice when Doug was ripped from my life. It decimated me. I had no choice but to lie in bed day after day. I couldn't choose to sleep, and I couldn't choose to wake up. I could barely talk, much less eat, shower, get dressed, or tend to my girls, whose heartbreak matched my own. That's why creating your Chosen Family and community is so important. That's why building resilience throughout your life is critical; someday, you'll need it. Resilience takes practice. It's like a muscle, and by making choices to support yourself, surrounding yourself with loving people, believing in yourself and your goals, and never giving up on love, that muscle will grow into a strength that you can rely on in good times and in the worst of times.

I worked so hard to build the perfect life, and I finally had it. Now I know that life is not perfect. I'm not perfect. I wasn't cut out to be a stay-at-home mom, but there I was, at least until I could build myself back up. I do the best I can, and that's a choice born of a lifetime of building resilience and grit, with one added ingredient: love. With all the support we received from my dearest friends and community, there came a day when I finally was able to get out of bed.

In addition to all that, I gave myself and the girls the therapeutic support we needed. We probably talk more about feelings than many families do, but, because of that, they are better able to express their sadness and their anger—and there's a lot of anger, as there should be. One of my girls, the nurturer, often wants to step into the caretaking role with me. I understand this. I took care of everyone in my family, and it was a burden. I don't want that to happen to her, so if she sees me broken and sad, I reassure her that Mommy is going to be okay and, though I appreciate her love, it's not her job to take care of me. She gets to be a little girl, and that's enough.

It's still messy and overwhelming at times, and I try to take short breaks by myself where I can recharge or simply unplug. It's not always easy to do, but it's necessary. Sitting at a restaurant bar, having a meal and a glass of wine, and not worrying about running into anyone I know is sometimes exactly what I need. The girls don't always like it when I take these breaks, but I tell them that a happy Mommy is a better Mommy. Still, I feel guilty. I feel guilty about everything. I feel guilty for trying to build this new life with the girls without Doug, but I know he would want this for me, and he would want this for our girls. But most of all, I know that he wanted to live this life along with us, to see his daughters grow up and experience all the special and ordinary moments of their lives, and to grow old with me. And that's what makes me feel the most guilty.

Sometimes, when I come back from a weekend away, or from a vacation, event or activity with my girls, I physically and emotionally crash. I find myself back in bed, immovable for a couple of days. This seems to be a part of the grief process, and I try to make room for it. For all of it. It's not about reestablishing normalcy. It's about creating a new and different kind of life in my own time. Nothing will take away the reality that Doug is gone. We can honor him, and we do, by talking about him, and our friends do the same. I honor him by doing everything in my power to make sure my girls have the life that Doug and I wanted them to have.

I may have been fueled by anger, but I want my girls to be fueled by our love for them. I want them to feel like they can do and be anything because of that love and the love they receive from our Chosen Family and community. That's what fuels me today. My story is not over, and theirs is just beginning.

Throughout my life, I talked myself into being a strong, resilient, iron-willed individual, and it worked—until now. I put on a brave face and, on the days that I can't, I don't fight it or apologize for it. Other than the love I have for my girls, I feel untethered. The drive, purpose, and fulfillment I experienced from work has vanished. Emptiness has taken its place. Grief has not only changed my brain, it has irrevocably changed my heart. It does not get better with time. As Elisabeth Kübler Ross, the Swiss-American psychiatrist and pioneer in grief research, wrote (along with David Kessler): "The reality is that you will grieve forever. You will not 'get over' the loss of a loved one; you will learn to live with it. You will heal and you will rebuild yourself around the loss you have suffered. You will be whole again but you will never be the same. Nor should you be the same, nor would you want to."

So, who am I now? Changed forever. Vulnerable. Deeply sensitive. Fiercely protective of my girls.

In the face of all this, I learn to live around it. Doug opened my heart forever, and now I'm on a different path. My former drive for work has softened into focusing on activities and work that are deeply personal to me, that are inspired by the oppression, intolerance, ignorance, and grief that I have experienced. I joined the board of a nonprofit group founded by bereaved parents that works to end preventable stillbirths. I do this because I know that, with my experience, both professionally and personally, I will be able to help them. Because I know what it's like to not have support, I also have become a Limited Partner in a venture capital fund that helps female founders succeed because I know what it's like not to have support. I've joined the board of an executive women's collective that uses leadership, investment, and philanthropy to drive cultural impact for women. And, I'm a member of a private business networking organization for senior women executives. I do these things with the same determination I have had throughout my life. And most of all, I do them for my girls so they learn that women support each other, that women should have each other's backs, and that women are a powerful community when you have the right ones in your life. This is who I am now. A woman fueled by resilience, love, and grit. A woman who loves her girls. A woman who loves and grieves the loss of her husband. A woman who loves her Chosen Family and community. Together, we can get through anything.

We can, we will, and we must.

ACKNOWLEDGMENTS

ALTHOUGH THIS IS THE story of my life, it's not just about me. It's also about the beautiful people in my life who choose to love me and my family: my Chosen Family.

Over the course of my teens, young adulthood and midlife, Lisa (Misciagna) Virga always told me I should save my stories and write a book about my life. I wish she could have read this memoir, but I'm forever grateful that she was and always will be part of my story. I am also indebted to Fran Misciagna, who was a second mother to me then and now, and to "our boys," James and Alex, who connect our lives into the next generation.

From the moment my husband, Doug, met my mother for the first time, I felt validated, heard, and seen. He is the one who filled the emptiness in my heart and made me whole. And because he knew my mother, he also encouraged me to write a book about how I accomplished all I had, despite my upbringing. Because of our family lives, we completed each other on almost a cellular level. I am who I am today in a very large part thanks to him, including making my dream of becoming a mother to my beautiful girls come true.

Thank you to the wonderful men in my professional life who championed me, believed in me and helped me thrive throughout my career: the late Brian Morris and Paul McDade, David Hung, Jayson Dallas, and Mark McDade. Each of you made an impact on my life and livelihood, and I am in your debt.

I've placed a heavy burden on Ed Broughton. Despite your own grief, you honor Doug in the most profound way. There are no words for your devotion and kindness; my gratitude is boundless.

Stephanie Koze, Andrea Ashford-Hicks, Linda Herman, and Carrie Steins, thank you for being my soul sisters through the decades. You are now and always will be my sisters of the heart. Mary Allen Cavanagh, know that you will always be my BFTWKTB.

Sarena Bains Khatri, Roshan Khatri, Abby Reyes, and Jon Owens intimately bear the incompleteness of life without Doug but step up to support and love the girls and me to keep us going every day. Leanne Shively took on an impossibly difficult task with love and empathy and will always be "Granny" to us all.

Chelle and Carl Tuttle and Veronica Wolf and Andrés White hold esteemed Auntie and Uncle roles for helping us endure the worst thing that can happen in life by simply being there and loving us. Ronny Brazdil, Gareth Hicks, and Ray Lynch, thank you for being Daddies since my girls can't have theirs.

I'll forever be thankful to Ramona Martz for the significant role you've played in helping us rebuild our broken family with love and patience, while upending your own. Meine tochter.

My Chosen Family loves our girls in a way all children should feel loved, as part of a community, a village, a great, big extended family. My gratitude goes out to so many who helped take care of the girls when I simply could not: Ene Siong and Thai Pham, Janel Riley and Ryan Talbot, Valda and Warren Sanders, Lamont and Valerie Brown, Tina and Gerard Collier, Divya and Prem Viswanathan, Ronny and Heidi Oatis, Thaïs Zayas-Bazán, Anderson Sanchez, the late Dirksen Rogers, and so many others in our wonderful community for being there to pick me up off the floor.

This is my story, but each of you is part of it. Thank you.

ABOUT THE AUTHOR

SAMINA BARI is a powerhouse in the biopharmaceutical industry and an inspiring leader who has never shied away from breaking barriers. With over 30 years of experience, and involvement in high-profile acquisitions collectively valued at over $40 billion, Samina has helped transform companies and paved the way for future generations of women leaders. As a first-generation American, she has faced her share of challenges, straddling cultural expectations while forging her own path in a life and an industry dominated by men. She's a fierce champion for women supporting women, actively mentoring and sponsoring women to help them rise in their careers and gain more board seats, and ensuring their success through investments in women-founded and owned companies. Through her writing, she's sharing her journey of overcoming adversity and finding strength in the face of unimaginable challenges—a message that resonates with anyone striving to make their mark against the odds. More at saminabari.com.